Creative Impulse
in Industry

This is a volume in the Arno Press collection

WORK

Its Rewards
and
Discontents

Advisory Editor

Leon Stein

*See last pages of this volume
for a complete list of titles*

CREATIVE IMPULSE IN INDUSTRY

HELEN MAROT

ARNO PRESS

A New York Times Company

New York / 1977

101516

Editorial Supervision: ANDREA HICKS

———◆———

Reprint Edition 1977 by Arno Press Inc.

Reprinted from a copy in
 The Princeton University Library

WORK: Its Rewards and Discontents
ISBN for complete set: 0-405-10150-3
See last pages of this volume for titles.

Manufactured in the United States of America

———◆———

Library of Congress Cataloging in Publication Data

Marot, Helen, 1865-1940.
  Creative impulse in industry.

    Reprint of the ed. published by Dutton, New York.
    1. Technical education--United States. 2. La-
bor and laboring classes--Education--United States.
3. Industry and education--United States.
I. Title.
LC1081.M28 1977   370.11'3'0973   77-70514
ISBN 0-405-10183-X

CREATIVE IMPULSE IN INDUSTRY

A Proposition for Educators

BY

HELEN MAROT
AUTHOR OF "AMERICAN LABOR UNIONS"

NEW YORK
E. P. DUTTON & COMPANY
681 FIFTH AVENUE

TO

CAROLINE PRATT

WHOSE APPRECIATION OF EDUCATIONAL FACTORS IN THE PLAY WORLD OF CHILDREN, INTENSIFIED FOR THE AUTHOR THE SIGNIFI-CANCE OF THE GROWTH PROCESSES IN INDUSTRIAL AND ADULT LIFE.

PREFACE

The Bureau of Educational Experiments is a group of men and women who are trying to face the modern problems of education in a scientific spirit. They are conducting and helping others to conduct experiments which hold promise of finding out more about children as well as how to set up school environments which shall provide for the children's growth. From these experiments they hope eventually may evolve a laboratory school.

Among their surveys the past year, one by Helen Marot has resulted in this timely and significant book. The experiment which is outlined at the close seems to the Bureau to be of real moment,—one of which both education and industry should take heed. They earnestly hope it may be tried immediately. In that event, the Bureau hopes to work with Miss Marot in bringing her experiment to completion.

The Bureau of Educational Experiments,
16 West Eighth Street,
New York City.

CONTENTS

CREATIVE IMPULSE IN INDUSTRY

INTRODUCTION

A FRIEND of mine in describing the Russian people as he observed them in their present revolution said it was possible for them to accept new ideas because they were uneducated; they did not, he said, labor under the difficulty common among educated people of having to get rid of old ideas before they took on new ones. I think what he had in mind to say was that it is difficult to accept new ideas when your mind is filled with ideas which are institutional. The ideas which come out of formal education, out of the schools, out of books, are ideas which have been stamped as the true and important ones; many of them are, as they have proved their worth in service. But as they represent authority, they pass into a people's mind with the full weight of an accepted fact. The schools, the colleges, and the books are not responsible primarily for the fixed ideas; every established institution contributes fixed ideas as well as fixed customs and rules of action. The schools and colleges circulate and interpret them. The movement for industrial education in the United States is an illustration of this.

The ideas which we find there have not sprung from schools or colleges but from industry. The institution of industry, rather than the institution of education, dominates thought in industrial education courses. It is the institution of industry as it has affected the life of every man, woman and child, which has inhibited educational thought in conjunction with schemes for industrial schools. No established system of education or none proposed is more circumscribed by institutionalized thought than the vocational and industrial school movement.

Educators have opposed the desire of business to attach the schools to the industrial enterprise. They have rightly opposed it because industry under the influence of business prostitutes effort. Nevertheless, hand in hand with industry, the schools must function; unattached to the human hive they are denied participation in life. Promoters of industrial education are hung up between this fact of prostituted industry and their desire to establish the children's connection with life. They have tried to meet opposing interests; they have not recognized all the facts because the facts were conflicting, and their minds as well as their interests, institutionally speaking, were committed to both.

This was the impasse we had apparently reached when the war occurred; it is where we still are. But ahead of us, sometime, the war will end and we shall be called then to face a period of reconstruction. The reconstruction will center around industry. The efficiency with which a worker serves industry will be the test of his patriotic fervor, as his service in the army is made the test during this time of war. All institutions will be examined and called upon to reorganize in such ways as will contribute to the enterprise of raising industrial processes to the standard of greatest efficiency.

The standard of mechanical efficiency as it was set by Germany was one of refined brutality. During the progress of the war, the significance of that standard is being grafted into the consciousness of the common people of those nations which have opposed Germany in arms. It is the industrial efficiency of Germany, uninhibited by a sense of human development that has made her victories possible. It is that efficiency which has kept a large part of the world on the defensive for over three and a half years. Germany's military strategy is, in the main, her industrial strategy; it represents her efficiency in turning technology to the account of an imperial purpose.

But those organizations of manufacturers and business politicians who believe that the same schemes of efficiency will function in America will call upon the people after the war, it is safe to predict, to emulate the methods which have given Germany its untoward strength. While it is these methods which have made much hated Germany a menace to the world and while the menace is felt by our own people, the significance of the methods is but vaguely realized. It is probable that after the war it will be said that it was not the German methods which were objectionable, but that it was their use in an international policy. Before the time for reconstruction comes, I hope we shall discover how intrinsically false those methods are; and how untrue to the growth process is the sort of efficiency Germany has developed. I hope also that we shall realize that a policy of paternalism has no place in the institutional life of our own country. Before the war these German methods bore the character of high success, and they had a large following in this country. There are indeed many thousands of men and women in the United States, who, while giving all they most care for, for the prosecution of the war against Germany still support industrial and political policies and dogmas which are in spirit essentially Prussian. The professional Reformer here in America is not even yet fully conscious that German paternalism (a phase of German efficiency) is the token of an enslaved people.

The German educational system as much if not more than its other imperial schemes has been instrumental in developing the German brand of industrial efficiency. The perfection in Germany of its technological processes is made possible as the youth of the country has been consecrated and sacrificed to the development of this perfection in the early years of school training. Parents contribute their children freely to an educational system which fits them into an industrial institution which has an imperial destiny to fulfill. Each person's place in the life of the nation is made for him during his early years, like a predestined fact.

American business men before the war ap-

preciated the educational system which made
people over into workers without will or purpose of their own. But the situation was em-
barrassing as these business men were not in a
position to insist that the schools, supported by
the people, should prepare the children to serve
industry for the sake of the state, while industry was pursued solely for private interest.
Their embarrassment, however, will be less
acute under the conditions of industrial reconstruction which will follow the war. Then as
patriots, under the necessity of competing with
Germany industrially, they will feel free to urge
that the German scheme of industrial education,
possibly under another name, be extended here
and adopted as a national policy. In other
words as Germany has evolved its methods of
attaining industrial efficiency, and as the schools
have played the leading part in the attainment,
the German system of industrial education, private business may argue, should be given for
patriotic reasons full opportunity in the United
States. If the German system were introduced
here, of course it is not certain that it could
deliver wage workers more ready and servile,
less single-purposed in their industrial activity
than they are now. It was in Germany a com-

paratively simple matter for the schools to make over the children into effective and efficient servants, for, as Professor Veblen explains, the psychology of the German people was still feudal when the modern system of industry, with its own characteristic enslavement, was imposed, ready-made, upon them; the German people unlike the Anglo-Saxon had not experienced the liberating effects of the political philosophy which developed along with modern technology in both England and America.*

First, then, it is not certain that the system of German industrial education would succeed; and, second, if it did succeed it is not the sort of education that America wants.

America wants industrial efficiency, it must have efficient workers if it holds its place among nations, and American people will prove their efficiency or their inefficiency as they are capable of using the heritage which industrial evolution has given the world. But what shall we use this efficiency for? For the sake of the heritage? For the sake of business? For the sake of Empire?

Business knows very clearly why it wants

---

* Thorstein Veblen—Imperial Germany and the Industrial Revolution.

it, but as a rule most of us are not clearly conscious that we need, for the sake of our expansive existence, to be industrially efficient. We are not even conscious that industry is the great field for adventure and growth, because we use that field not for the creative but for the exploitive purpose.

It is the present duty of American educators to realize these two points: that industry is the great field for adventure and growth; that as it is used now the opportunities for growth are inhibited in the only field where productive experience can be a common one. Shortly it will be the mission of educators to show that by opening up the field for creative purpose, fervor for industrial enterprise and good workmanship may be realized; that only as the content of industry in its administration as well as in the technique of its processes is opened up for experiment and first-hand experience, will a universal impulse for work be awakened. It is for educators, together with engineers and architects, to demonstrate to the world that while the idea of service to a political state may have the power to accomplish large results, all productive force is artificially sustained which is not dependent on men's desire to do creative work. A state as we have seen, may invoke the idea of service. It might represent the productive interests of a community if those interests sprang from the expansive experience of a people in their creative adventures.

In the reconstructive period educators may have their opportunity to extend the concept that the creative process is the educative process, or as Professor Dewey states it, the educative process is the process of growth. The reconstruction period will be a time of formative thought; institutions will be attacked and on the defensive; and out of the great need of the nations there may come change. Educators will find their opportunity as they discover conditions under which the great enterprise of industry may be educational and as they repudiate or oppose institutions which exclude educational factors.

It is for educators to realize first of all that there can be no social progress while there is antagonism between growth in wealth (which is industry) and growth in individuals (which is education); that the fundamental antagonisms which are apparent in the current arrangement are not between industry and education but between education and business. They must know that as business regulates and controls industry for ulterior purposes, that is for other purposes than production of goods, it thwarts the development of individual lives and the evolution of society; that it values a worker not for his potential productivity but for his immediate contribution to the annual stock dividend; or if, as in Germany where his productive potentiality is valued in terms of longer time, it is for the imperial intention of the state and not for the growth of the individual or the progress of civilization.

CREATIVE IMPULSE IN INDUSTRY

CHAPTER I

PRODUCTION AND CREATIVE EFFORT

As a human experience, the act of creating, the process of fabricating wealth, has been at different times as worthy of celebration as the possession of it. Before business enterprise and machine production discredited handwork, art for art's sake, work for the love of work, were conceivable human emotions. But to-day, a Cezanne who paints pictures and leaves them in the field to perish is considered by the general run of people, in communities inured to modern industrial enterprise, as being not quite right in his head. Their estimate is of course more or less true. But such valuations are made without the help of creative inspiration, although the functioning of a product has its

1

creative significance. The creative significance of a product in use, as well as an appreciation of the act of creating, would be evident if modern production of wealth, under the influence of business enterprise and machine technology, had not fairly well extinguished the appreciation and the joy of creative experience in countries where people have fallen under its influence so completely as in our own.

It is usual in economic considerations to credit the period of craftsmanship as a time in the evolution of wealth production that was rich in creative effort and opportunity for the individual worker. The craftsmanship period is valued in retrospect for its educative influence. There was opportunity then as there is not now for the worker to gain the valuable experience of initiating an idea and carrying the production of an article to its completion for use and sale in the market; there was the opportunity then also as there is not now, for the worker to gain a high degree of technique and a valuation of his workmanship. It is characteristic of workmanship that its primary consideration is serviceability or utility. The creative impulse and the creative effort may or may not express workmanship or take it into account.

Workmanship in its consideration of service-ability oftentimes arrives at beauty and classic production, when creative impulse without the spirit of workmanship fails. The craftsmanship period deserves rank, but the high rank which is given it is due in part to its historical relation to the factory era which followed and crushed it. While craftsmanship represented expansive development in workmanship, it is not generally recognized that the Guild organization of the crafts developed modern business enterprise.* Business is concerned wholly with utility, and not like workmanship, with standards of production, except as those standards contain an increment of value in profits to the owners of wealth. It was during the Guild period that business came to value workmanship because it contained that increment. In spite of business interest, however, the standard of workmanship was set by skilled craftsmen, and their standards represented in a marked degree the market value of the goods produced by them.

While the exploitation of the skill of the workman in the interest of the owners of raw materials and manufactured goods, had its de-

* Thorstein Veblen; Instinct of Workmanship, pp. 211-212.

pressing and corrupting influence on creative effort, the creative impulse found a stimulus in the respect a community still paid the skill and ability of the worker. It was not until machine standards superseded craft standards and discredited them that the processes of production, the acts of fabrication, lost their standards of workmanship and their educational value for the worker. The discredits were psychological and economic; they revolutionized the intellectual and moral concepts of men in relation to their work and the production of wealth.

As machine production superseded craftsmanship the basis of fixing the price of an article shifted from values fixed by the standards of workers to standards of machines, Professor Veblen says to standards of salesmen. It is along these lines that mechanical science applied to the production of wealth, has eliminated the personality of the workers. A worker is no longer reflected in goods on sale; his personality has passed into the machine which has met the requirements of mass production.

The logical development of factory organization has been the complete coördination of all factors which are auxiliary to mechanical power and devices. The most important auxiliary factor is human labor. A worker is a perfected factory attachment as he surrenders himself to the time and the rhythm of the machine and its functioning; as he supplements without loss whatever human faculties the machine lacks, whatever imperfection hampers the machine in the satisfaction of its needs. If it lacks eyes, he sees for it; he walks for it, if it is without legs; and he pulls, drags, lifts, if it needs arms. All of these things are done by the factory worker at the pace set by the machine and under its direction and command. A worker's indulgence in his personal desires or impulses hinders the machine and lowers his attachment value.

This division of the workers into eyes, arms, fingers, legs, the plucking out of some one of his faculties and discarding the rest of the man as valueless, has seemed to be an organic requirement of machine evolution. So commendable the scheme has been to business enterprise that this division of labor has been carried from the machine shop and the factory to the scientific laboratories where experiment and discovery in new processes of technology are developed, and where, it is popularly supposed, a high order of intelligence is required. The organization of technological laboratories, like the organization of construction shops to which they are auxiliary, is based on the breaking up of a problem which is before the laboratory for its solution. The chemists, physicists, machinists and draftsmen are isolated as they work out their assigned tasks without specific knowledge of what the general problem is and how it is being attacked. Small technological laboratories are still in existence where the general problem in hand is presented as a whole to the whole engineering staff, and is left to them as a group for independent and associated experimentation. But even in such cases the technological content does not necessarily supply the impulse to solve the problem or secure a free and voluntary participation in its solution. Those who are interested in its solution are inspired by its economic value for them. In all technological laboratories, either where the problem is broken up and its parts distributed among the employees of the laboratory, or where it is given to them as a whole for solution, it is given not as a sequence in the creative purpose of the individuals who are at work on it, nor is its final solution necessarily determined by its use and wont in a community.

Problems brought to the laboratory are tainted with the motive of industry which is not creative, but exploitive.

The tenure of each man employed in production is finally determined not by any creative interest of his own or of his employer but by whether in the last analysis, he conforms better than another man to the exigencies of profits. If profits and creative purpose happen to be one and the same thing, his place in an industrial establishment has some bearing on his intrinsic worth. Under such circumstances his interest in the creative purpose of the establishment would have a foundation, and he himself could value better than he otherwise would his own part in the enterprise.

The economic organization of modern society though built on the common people's productive energy has discounted their *creative potentiality*. We hold to the theory that men are equal in their opportunity to capture and own wealth; that their ability in that respect is proof of their ability to create it; a proof of their inherent capacity. It is a proof, as a matter of fact, of their ability to compete in the general scheme of capture; their ability to exploit wealth successfully. While the prevailing economic *theory* of production takes for granted men's creative *potentiality* there is no provision in our industrial institution for the common run of men to *function* creatively. There is no attempt in the general scheme for trueing-up or estimating the creative ability of workers. In the market, where the value of goods is determined, a machine tender has a better chance than a craftsman. The popular belief is that the ability of workers has native limitations, that these limitations are absolute and that they are fixed at or before birth. This belief is a tenet among those who hold positions of industrial mastery. Managers of industry for instance who control a situation and create an environment, demand that those who serve them meet the requirements which they have fixed. They do not recognize that industrial ability depends largely on the opportunity which an individual has had to make adjustments to his surroundings and on his opportunity to master them through experiment. A factory employee is required to do a piece of work; and he does it, not because he is interested in the process or the object, but because his employer wants it done.

In Anglo-Saxon and Teutonic countries,

where people have fallen most completely under the influence of machine production and business enterprise, and where they have lost by the way their conception of their creative potentiality, work is universally conceived as something which people endure for the sake of being "paid off." Being paid off, it seems abundantly clear, is the only reason a sane man can have for working. After he is paid off the assumption is his pleasure will begin. A popular idea of play is the absence of work, the consumption of wealth, being entertained. Being entertained indeed is as near as most adult men in these countries come to play. Their Sundays and holidays are depressing occasions, shadowed by a forlorn expectancy of something which never comes off.

The capacity of the French people for enjoying their holidays is much the same as their capacity for enjoying their work. This, no doubt, is a matter of native habituation. But however they came by it, it has had its part in determining the industrial conditions of France. The love of the people for making things has resisted in a remarkable way the domination of machine industry and modern factory organization. The French work shop, averaging six persons, is as characteristic of France as the huge factory organization with the most modern mechanical equipment is characteristic of American industry. As the workers in these shops participate more intimately in the fabrication of goods they come more nearly to a real participation in productive enterprise. This close contact with the actual processes of production gives the workers a sense of power. A sense of their relation to the processes and their ability to control them engenders courage. Indeed it is the absence of fear, rather than the absence of work, that determines the capacity of men for play.

It was not accidental that the movement of the French workers for emancipation emphasized a desire for control of industry. The syndicalism of France has expressed the workers' interest in production as the labor movements of other countries have laid stress exclusively on its economic value to them. The syndicalists' theory takes for granted the readiness of workers to assume responsibility for production, while the trade unionists of England, Germany and the United States ask for a voice in determining not their productive but their financial relation to it.

It is the habit of these other peoples to credit the lack of interest in work to physical hardships which the wage system has imposed. But the wage system from the point of view of material welfare has borne no less heavily on the French than on other workers. It is also difficult to prove that the physical hardships of modern methods of production are greater than the hardships of earlier methods. The truth is that neither hardships nor exploitation of labor are new factors; they have both, through long centuries, repressed in varying degree the inspirational and intellectual interest of workers in productive effort. It is not the economic burdens which followed the introduction of machinery and the division of labor that distinguish these new factors in industry, but the discredit which they throw around man's labor power. They have carried the discredit of labor in its social position further than it had been carried, but this is merely a by-product of the discredit they cast on the skill and intellectual power which is latent in the working class. In this connection the significant truth for civilization is that while exploitation of labor and physical hardships induce the antagonism between labor and capital, modern factory organization destroys creative desire and individual initiative as it excludes the workers from participation in creative experience.

The new discoveries in inorganic power and their application to industrial enterprise are possibly more far reaching in their effect on the adjustment and relationships of men than they have been at any other time in the last century and a half. Whatever the world owes to these discoveries and their applications it cannot afford to lose sight of a fact of great social significance, which is, that people have accepted mechanical achievements, not as labor saving devices but as substitutes for human initiative and effort. They have not, indeed, saved labor to the advantage of labor itself, and they have inhibited interest in production. Outside of business enterprise and diplomacy—the political extension of business—mechanical devices have lost the surprise reaction and resentment which they originally set up. As a competitor with human labor they have established themselves as its fit survivor. The prophesy of Theophrastus Such seems to have been already fulfilled, and any new machine added to those already in power in the Parliament of Machines can scarcely add to the worker's sense of his own impotency. The business valuations which were evolved out of craftsmanship and which were further developed under the influence of the technology of the last century and a half, emphasized the value of material force, and repressed spiritual evaluations, such as the creative impulse in human beings.

Modern industrial institutions are developed by an exclusive cultivation of people's needs and the desire to possess. They are developed independently, as we have seen, of any need or desire to create. The desire to possess is responsible for the production of a mass of goods unprecedented and inconceivable a century and a half ago. The actual production of all of these goods is unrelated to the motive of men's participation in their production; the actual production in relation to the motive is an incident. The sole reason for the participation in the productive effort is not the desire for creative experience or the satisfaction of the creative impulse; it is not an interest in supplying the needs of a community or in the enrichment of life; it is to acquire out of the store of goods all that can be acquired for personal possession or consumption. There is no more fundamental need than the need to consume; but for the common run of men as a motive in the creation of wealth, it is shorn of adventure, of imagination and of joy.

The ownership of many things, which mass production has made possible, the intensive cultivation of the desire to own, has added another element to the corruption of workmanship and the depreciation of its value. Access to a mass of goods made cheap by machinery has had its contributing influence in the people's depreciation of their own creative efforts. As people become inured to machine standards, they lose their sense of art values along with their joy in creative effort, their self regard as working men and their personal equation in industrial life.

Where the motive of individuals who engage in industry is the desire to possess, the rational method of gaining possession is not by the arduous way of work but of capture. The scheme of capture is a scheme whereby you may get something for (doing) nothing; nothing as nearly as possible in the way of fabrication of goods; something for the manipulation of men; something for the development of technology and mechanical science; and high regard for the manipulation of money. "Doing nothing" does not mean that manual workers, managers of productive enterprises, speculators in the natural resources of wealth production and manufactured goods, as well as financiers, are not busy people, or that their activity does not result in accomplishment. They are indeed *the* busy people and their accomplishment is the world's wealth. Nevertheless the intention of all and the spirit of the scheme is to do as near nothing as possible in exchange for the highest return. *The whole industrial arrangement is carried on without the force of productive intention; it is carried forward against a disinclination to produce.*

I have said that industry was shorn of adventure for the common man. Adventure in industrial enterprise is the business man's great monopoly. His impetus is not due to his desire to create wealth but to exploit it, and he secures its creation by "paying men off." Commonly he is peevishly expectant that those he pays off will have a creative intention toward the work he pays them to do, although in the scheme of industry which he supports the opportunity provided for such intention is negligible. An efficiency engineer estimated that there is a loss in wealth of some fifty per cent, due to the inability of the business man to appraise the creative possibilities in industry.

When exploitation of wealth is referred to, those who own it are generally meant. But exploitation of wealth is the intention of the worker as well as of the business man. To get, as I have said, something for (doing) nothing is the dominating *motif* in the industrial world. It is supposed to reflect the self-interest of individuals, to reflect, that is, their economic needs.

This motive of circumscribed self-interest during an era of political and industrial expansion has been adopted by philosophers as the guide as well as a clue to conduct; it was hailed by them as a sufficient and complete motivation for wealth creation; they used it as a basis of a theory for race progress resting solely on the efforts of men to satisfy their material needs through their ability to capture goods. This motive together with the possibilities which machine production opened up for wealth exploitation, gave birth to the dismal science of Political Economy; it suggested the materialistic interpretation of history, and brought to earth utopian schemes of brotherhood. Political science is dismal because it is an interpretation of dismal institutions. It may be ungenerous to speak slightingly of institutions which have yielded such great wealth, which have transformed inert matter into productive power and brought in consequence the whole world into acquaintanceship and rivalry. It would be ungenerous if it were not for a fact which has become poignant, that the exploitation of wealth and undigested relationships are to-day the outstanding menace to civilization.

The present world conflict has made it clear that relationships cannot remain undigested; that they are not in their nature passive. They are either integrating in their force or disintegrating. Socialism has undertaken for two generations to prove that exploitation carries with it its own seeds of destruction. The position of the socialists is passing out of theory and propaganda through the hands of diplomatists, into statutes. Both the socialists and their successors would eradicate exploitation by repressing it. The socialists would repress it by shifting ownership of wealth from individuals to the state, while the diplomatists, through the same agency, would regulate those who own it.

It is an historical fact as well as a psychological one that you do not get rid of traits or institutions except as you replace them with something of positive service, or greater competitive value. The institution of capitalism exists not because of its predatory character, but because in spite of its exploitation it *promotes* industry, and labor and other industrial technicians do not. As our industrial institutions have grown out of a predatory concept instead of a creative one, as capture has been rewarded rather than work, as the possessive desire has been stimulated and the creative desire has been sacrificed, as employers of men and owners of machines have engaged in production because of their interest not in the process or in the use of the product, but in the reward, as wage workers have hired out for the day's work or continued during their adult life in their trade without interest in its development, because like their employers they wanted the highest cash return, wealth exploitation has come to be synonymous in the minds of men with wealth creation. A creative concept which could survive and inhibit the predatory concept must rest on such elements of creative force as are now absent from our industrial institution.

It is almost axiomatic to say that a system of wealth production which cultivated creative effort would yield more in general terms of life as well as in terms of goods, than a system like our own which exploits creative power. It is obvious that the disintegrating tendency in our system is due to the fact that production is dependent for its motive force on the desire to possess. It is also obvious that a rational system of industry which sought to give that desire among all men full opportunity for satisfaction would also undertake to cultivate the creative impulse for the sake of increasing creative effort   The result would be an increase in production. As logical as this observation may be, it is not so obvious how such a social transformation as this implies, may be effected.

Every advance in wealth creation which has become an institutional part of an economic system has been impelled and sustained by the material interests of people who at the time held the strategic position in the community. The world has progressed, or retrogressed, as the most powerful interests at any time adjusted the institutions and customs governing wealth production to their own advantage. As the controlling interests in our present scheme are the business interests, it is the business man, not the workman, who directs industry and determines its policy as well as the general policy of the nation in which it operates. It is to the advantage of private business run for private gain, to control creative effort for the purpose of appropriating the product, and to inhibit free creative expression as an uncontrollable factor in the enterprise of exploitation.

The appalling and wanton sacrifice of life which are incident to the evolution of machinery and the division of labor seem to demand at times their elimination. In weariness we are urged to retrace our steps and go back to craftsmanship and the Guilds. But it is idle to talk about going back or eliminating institutionalized features of society. We cannot go back, we have not the ability to discard this or that part of our environment except as we make it over. The result of this making over might be vitalized by methods which had belonged to earlier periods, but neither the methods nor the periods, we can safely say, will live again. Neither our own nor future generations will escape the influence of modern technology. It will play its part. It may be a part which will lead away from some of the destructive influences which developed in the era of craftsmanship and which dominate the present. But a society too enfeebled to use its own experience will not have the power to use the experience of another people or of another time. It is beside the point to look to some other experience or scheme of life and choose that because it seems good, unless the choice is based on a people's present fitness to adapt that other experience or other scheme of life to their own experience. The proposition to revert to an earlier period suggests nothing more than the repetition of an experience out of which the present state of affairs has evolved.

Nor is there ground for the hope that in time institutions and relationships will be regulated on principles of altruism. It is not apparent indeed that such regulations would yield even the present allowance of happiness incident to our own immature method of capturing what wealth we can without relation to social factors. As unfortunate as we are in pursuit of that blind method, it is safe to predict that the world would be a madder place than it is to-day if every one devoted himself to doing what he believed was for the good of everybody else.

The hope of social revolutionists that private

business would overreach itself and defeat its own purpose, grew out of the expectation that its tribute exactions would draw the subjects of capital together in a common defensive movement; that the movement on account of its numbers would overturn business and that in place of private management democratic control would be instituted. Some such outcome, sooner or later, seems inevitable if civilization is scheduled to advance. The labor union movement, unlike the political socialist revolutionary movement, undertakes in its operation to supply labor with a certain working content, which the administrative scheme of industry has excluded from the experience of its workers. But this content is not sufficient to stimulate the imagination of the trade unionists with the thought that the world of industry is the field of creative adventure. Their conception born of experience is not so flattering. It would be a brave man who would undertake to convince the twentieth century adult wage earner, involved in modern methods of machine production, that his poverty is less in his possession of wealth than in his growth and in his creative opportunity.

The industrial changes which the labor movement proposes to make are on the side of a better distribution of goods. A better distribution would have a dynamic significance in wealth production, if the actual increase which labor secured in wages and leisure were a real increase. But exploiting capital provides for such exigencies as high wages by increasing the price of products, thus reducing the wage earners' purchasing power to the former level. High wages fail to disturb the relative position of capital and labor even more than they fail to affect the purchasing power of the worker.

It is often suggested that if the state assumed control of industry the blight of business could be removed. But in the transfer we would not necessarily gain opportunity to enjoy the adventure which industry holds out. Industry as a creative experience, it is safe to predict, would be as rare a personal experience and as foreign an influence in social existence under state management as it is under business management. The state would curb the amount of wealth exploitation possibly, but would not alter the universal attitude toward wealth production, which is to take as much and give as little as one can get off with.

Although political socialism may be the economic sequel of private capital there is no foundation for the belief that it will of itself induce creative effort or stimulate creative impulse. The faith back of the socialist movement that desirable attributes like the creative impulse, which men potentially possess, will begin to operate automatically and universally as soon as there is sufficient leisure and food for general consumption, is blind and historically unwarranted. The signs are that a socialist state would lean exclusively on the consumption desire for production results, just as the present system of business now does. Neither fat incomes nor large leisure have furnished the world with its people of genius. In spite of the inhibiting influence of exploitation, they have come, what there are of them, out of intensive application to some matter of moment. Possibly they would come, and more of them, from the work-a-day world under socialism with the inhibiting influence of organized exploitation removed, but more of them would not insure a democracy in industry or elsewhere. Nothing insures that short of a strong emotional impulse, a real intellectual interest in the adventure of productive enterprise.

The creative desire is an incident or a sort of

by-product of the economics of socialism as it is of classical economics; neither one nor the other depends on its cultivation. Either is capable of achieving mass production, but neither insures a democratic control of industry, neither provides for growth, for education in the productive process. A democracy of industry requires a people's sustained interest in the productive enterprise; their interest in the development of technology, the development of markets, and the release of man's productive energy.

It happens that in machine production and in the division of labor there are emotional and intellectual possibilities which were non-existent in the earlier and simpler methods of production. As power latent in inorganic matter has been freed and applied to common needs, an environment has been evolved, filled with situations incomparably more dramatic than the provincial affairs of detached people and communities. Although this technological subject matter, rich in opportunities for associated adventure and infinite discovery, is not a part of common experience, it exists, and if called out from its isolation for purposes of common experimentation, it is fit matter for making science a vital experience in the productive life of the worker.

Industry under the direction of business will not open up the adventure with its stimulating factors to its subservient labor force, unless it happens that the present methods fail, in time, to carry forward industrial enterprise on a profit-making basis; or unless labor develops the power which springs from desire for creative experience, to undertake the direction and control of industry.

The present is better than any time earlier in the history of technology for the development of a concept of industry as a socially creative enterprise. As craftsmanship extended and intensified an interest in personal ownership, it magnified the value of possessions; as it deepened the desire for protection of private property and the strengthening of property laws against human laws, it was not a *socializing* force. While the craftsmanship period strengthened personal claims on workmanship and interest in it, mechanical power and division of labor have impersonalized industry.* In the labyrinth of mechanical processes and economic calculation it is not to-day possible for a worker

* Thorstein Veblen—Instinct of Workmanship, Chapter V.

10/5/6

to think or speak of a product as his. He has no basis for ownership claims in any article; even the price is arranged between buyer and seller and he is not the seller. An article owes its existence to an infinite number of persons and its place in the market to as many more.

A worker's claim to the product of his labor is merged in an infinity of claims which makes the product more nearly the property of society than of any one individual. And this merging of claims which has resulted in the submerging of all wage workers, has set up the new educational task of discovering the possibilities for creative experience in associated enterprise.

While an article manufactured under business conditions is the product of enforced association, we have in this condition the mechanics of a real association. As it now stands, the association is one of individuals, with the impulse for association and for creative effort left out. The interests of some ninety workers associated together in the making of a shoe are not common but antagonistic, except as they are common in their antagonism to the owner of the shoe on which they work. They hang together because they must; their parting is the best part of a working day.

And yet the practice of dividing up the fabrication of an article among the members of a group instead of confining the making of it to one or two people, opens up the possibility of extensive social intercourse, and has the power, we may discover, to sublimate the inordinate desire for the intensive satisfaction of personal life. Although the division of labor has given us a society which is abortive in its functioning like a machine with half assembled parts, it offers us the mechanics for interdependence and the opportunity to work out a coördinated industrial life.

CHAPTER II

As machine power rivalled hand work, promoters of industry until recently relied for its advancement on the perfection of technology, giving little thought to the perfection of labor. It was confidently assumed that labor, out of its own necessities, would adapt itself automatically to the new requirements of the machine, and to the shifts of business interest. When it was discovered that there were limitations to labor's voluntary adaptation under the conditions laid down, intelligent business in America decided that the responsibility for realizing labor's adaptation or "labor's coöperation" as they call it, must be assumed by the management of industry and that that management must be scientifically worked out and applied.

Scientific management is scientific as it subjects the labor operations on each job, each specific job to be performed in a factory, to a test-

29

ing out of the energy consumed; to discovering how to secure labor's maximum productivity without waste of time or energy. It is scientific as the manager's state of mind towards the physical and psychological reactions of the workers is one of inquiry and a readiness to accept, as facts of mechanical science are accepted, the reaction of the workers. A scientific manager, or engineer as he is often called, bears the same relation to the labor force in a factory that an electrical engineer bears to the electrical equipment. If his attention to the emotional reaction of the workers is less detached than scientific standards require, it must be remembered that he is trying to make adjustments which must first of all meet definite business conditions. Where the reactions of the workers interfere with the whole scheme of business administration (and interfere they ceaselessly do), he has to substitute measures which are not strictly speaking scientific. On these occasions he adopts humanitarian schemes, which are generally spoken of as welfare work. It is the introduction of these schemes which look like a "slop over" from science to charity, that makes it difficult for outsiders to tell just what scientific management is and what it is not.

Mr. Frederick W. Taylor, the founder of scientific management, was capable of scientific detachment in studying working men in relation to the specific job. He was able more notably than others had been before him, and more than many who have followed him, to extend the impersonal state of mind, which he enjoyed in the study of inorganic energy, to his study of human energy. Mr. Taylor's interest did not emanate from sympathy with labor in its hardships; his interest was centered in an effort to conserve and apply labor energy with maximum economy for wealth production. Mr. Taylor awakened the consciousness of industrial managers to the fact that the energy of workers like the power of machinery is subject to laws. He demonstrated that it was possible in specific operations to discover how the highest degree of energy could be attained and the largest output result, without loss through fatigue. He showed how efficiency could be enhanced by transferring the responsibility of standards of work from the workers to the managers. He formulated, as a business and industry doctrine, that a definite relation between the expenditure of labor energy and the labor reward could be established; that the wage incentive, if applied to labor in relation to energy expended, would yield, or might be expected to yield increased returns. These incentives, rewards, stimuli, which employers could apply would produce, he stated with unscientific fervor, the workers' initiative. The inability of Mr. Taylor and other scientific managers to distinguish between initiative and short lived reaction to stimulus is simple evidence that their scientific experiments were confined to comparisons which they could make between a yield in wealth where the stimulus to labor is weak, and a yield where it is strong. They will not discover what a worker's productivity is, or might be, when incited by his impulse to work, nor will they secure labor's initiative, until they release the factors, latent in industry, which have inspirational, creative force.

The attitude of Mr. Taylor and his followers, however, differs from that of the ordinary manager who maintains an irritated disregard of the disturbing elements instead of accepting them and, as far as is consistent with business principles, allaying or cajoling them. The significant contributions which scientific management has made are in line with the experiments originally introduced by Mr. Taylor. They call for the study of each new task by the management, for discovering the economy in the expenditure of labor energy before it is submitted to the working force; the standardizing of the task in conformity with the findings; the teaching of the approved methods to the working force; the introduction of incentives which will insure the full response of labor in the accomplishment of the task. Beside the standardizing of tasks and the relating the wage to the fixed standard, scientific management has made intensive experiments in the scheduling of the various operations to be performed, which are divided among the working force, so that no one operation is held up awaiting the completion of another. It has shown in this connection that work can be "routed" so that the time of workers is not lost. The most successfully managed factories also plan their annual product so that employment will be continuous. They have discovered that the periods of unemployment seriously affect the personnel of a labor force and they estimate that the turnover of the labor force which requires the constant breaking in of new men is an item of serious financial loss. The Ford Automobile Works at one time hired 50,000 men in one year while not employing at any one time more than 14,000. They estimated that the cost of breaking in a new man averaged $70.00. To reduce this cost, they instituted profit sharing, as an incentive for men to remain. Other factories have estimated the cost of replacing men from $50.00 to $200.00. A rubber concern in Ohio has a labor turnover of 150 per cent. In connection with the effort to reduce the turnover in the labor force the management of well organized factories takes great care to estimate a worker's value before employing him. The policy of transferring a man from one department to another where he is better suited yields evidently valuable results. In factories where there is effort to hold labor, to make employment continuous, the turnover has been reduced in some cases to as low as 18 per cent. Generally, however, it is still high; frequently as high as 50 per cent, and 50 per cent is still considered low, even in factories which have given the subject much consideration.

There is a tendency in developing the mechanics of efficiency, as they relate to labor, to establish for machine production standards of workmanship. Long and weary experience has proved that wage earners under factory methods and machine conditions are not interested in maintaining standards of work. The standards which are set by the scientific management schemes of efficiency are not, to be sure, the qualitative standards of craftsmanship but they are qualitative as well as quantitative standards of machine work. The tendency to establish standards should have educational significance for workers. It would have, if the responsibility for setting standards as well as maintaining them rested in any measure with the workers; it would have, that is, if the workers had the interest in workmanship, which as things now stand they have not. The point in scientific management is that efficiency depends, wholly depends they believe, on centralizing the responsibility for setting and maintaining workmanship standards, on transferring the responsibility for standards of work from workers who do it, to the management who directs it done. I have learned of only one manager who realizes that although the factory workers are not to be trusted to maintain standards, a management nevertheless will fail to get the workers' full coöperation until it arouses their interest in maintaining them.

The manager is Mr. Robert Wolf, who illustrated this point at a meeting of the Taylor Society in March, 1917. In describing the process of extracting the last possible amount of water from paper pulp, he said:

"Our problem was to determine the best length of time to keep the low pressure on, as the high pressure is governed entirely by the production coming from the wet machine. After having determined that three minutes of low pressure . . . gives maximum moisture test, we furnished each man on the wet machines with a clock and asked him to leave this low pressure on just three minutes. As long as the foremen kept constantly after their men and vigilantly followed them up we obtained some slight increase in the test; but it required a constant urging upon our part to focus the attention of the men upon this three minute time of low pressure. . . . We realized finally that in order to get the results we were after, it was necessary for us to produce *a desire* upon the part of our men to do this work in the proper way . . . so we designed an instrument which would give us a record of the time lost between pressing operations, also the number of minutes the low pressure was kept on. It took us something over a year to perfect this machine, but after it was finally perfected and a record of the operations made, we found that the men actually were operating at an average efficiency of 42 per cent, and our moisture test was running about 54 per cent. Our next step was to post a daily record of the relative standing of the men in the machine room, put-

ting the men who had the best record at the top of
the list, in the order of their weekly average efficiencies. (The efficiency of low pressure, which proved to
be the most important factor, was computed by calling
three minutes of low pressure 100 per cent and two
minutes either way 0 per cent.) As a result of simply
posting this record our efficiencies rose to over 60 per
cent and our moisture test increased a little less than
1 per cent. Some of the best and most skilled men
had an efficiency of over 80 per cent, but quite a large
percentage of them were down below 50 per cent. We
therefore decided that it was necessary to have the
foreman give more detailed information to the men as
to what the machine meant and how their efficiencies
were obtained and to put the instrument which did
the recording into a glass case in the machine room
where all the men could see it. Each foreman took a
portion of the chart and one of the celluloid scales by
which we obtained the efficiencies and explained in
detail to each one of the men how their records were
calculated. As a result of this, our efficiency rose from
60 per cent to 80 per cent in less than four weeks, and
it has remained at 80 per cent ever since—(ever since
being over two years)—enabling us to get a moisture
of over 56 per cent." *

This was accomplished, Mr. Wolf told them,
without resorting to piece work or bonus or any
of the special methods of payments, their men
being hired by the day throughout the entire

* Bulletin of the Taylor Society—March, 1917.

plant. Mr. Wolf accomplished the result by giving meaning to a meaningless task, by letting the men see for themselves how they arrived at results, letting them see the different processes of getting results and knowing on their own account which were the most valuable.

There may be other managers who appreciate the value of letting men in on the experimental effort of getting results but it is not the practice to do so and it is opposed to the idea of transferring the responsibility from the workshop to the manager's office or laboratory. Because of this practice the educational value of establishing standards of workmanship is lost so far as the workers are concerned. Mr. Wolf's criticism of orthodox scientific management and his conclusions are illuminating; they are indeed revolutionary in nature as they come from a manager of a successful industrial enterprise:

"Our efforts, ever since we began to realize the workman's point of view, have been not to take responsibility from him. It is our plan to increase his responsibility and we feel that it is our duty to teach him to exercise his reasoning power and intelligence to its fullest extent. There is *no advantage gained by stimulating a man's reasoning power, and through this means his creative faculty, if the management relieves the man of the responsibility for each individual operation.* The opportunity for self expression, which is synonymous with joy in work, is something that the workman is entitled to, and we employers who feel that management is to become a true science must begin to think less of the science of material things and think more of the science of human relationships. Our industries must become *humanized,* otherwise there will be no relief from the present state of unrest in the industries of the world.

"In this connection it might be well to observe that our experience in the pulp industry has been that instructions which go *too much into detail* tend to deaden interest in the work. We realize fully the value of sufficient instructions to get uniform results, but we try to leave as much as possible to the judgment of the individual operator, making our instructions take more the form of constant *teaching of principles* involved in the operation than of definite *fixed rules* of procedure. It is necessary to produce a desire in the heart of the workman to do good work. No amount of coercion will enlist him thoroughly in the service.

"The new efficiency is going to reckon a great deal more with the needs of the individual man; but in order to do this, it must have some philosophical conception of the reason for man's existence. *It is beginning to be understood that when we deny to vast numbers of individuals the opportunity to do creative work, we are violating a great universal law.*"

Scientific management is sacrificing educational opportunity latent in the realization of workmanship standards in the same way that machinery sacrificed it. They both curtail the workers' chance to discover first-hand what the processes of fabrication are, the processes in which they are involved; they must adopt ready-made methods of doing their work, they must accept them out of hand without questioning, or chance to question, their validity. Workers endowed with good health and moral vigor resist these attempts to put something over on them, irrespective of their good or evil results.

The workers have resisted machinery not only because as individuals they were thrown out of jobs for a time or lost them permanently, but because the machine imposed on them a method of work, of activity over which they had no control. Scientific management has undertaken to gather up whatever bits of initiative the machine had not already taken over and to hand back to the workers at the bench directions for them to follow with a blind ability to accept instruction. It is incredible to factory managers that workers object to being taught ''right'' ways of doing things. Their objection is not to being taught, but to being told that

some one way is right without having had the
chance to know why, or whether indeed it is the
right way. This resistance to being taught, it
seems, is nothing more nor less than a wayward
desire of a worker to do his own way because
it is his way, and of course from the managers'
point of view, that is stupid. It is stupid, but
the stupidity is in the situation. What does
this waywardness of the worker to do his own
way suggest? Not that he has a way worth
bothering about but that he wants to exercise
the quality which all industrial managers agree
he does not possess—his initiative. Now a man
who has the desire to exercise initiative and does
not know how to put anything through is not
only a useless person in society but the most
pestiferous fellow in existence. Allowing that
he is does not mean that he has not the power
of initiative or that he could not have learned
to put this initiative to good use, if at any time
in his manhood or youth he had been taught to
use it, instead of being required to follow the
accepted ways of doing things without having
had the experience of trial and error. Schools
and factory management give workers scant opportunity to discover whether they have initiative or have not.

Mr. Wolf finds that "while it is possible, under certain conditions, to compel obedience, there is no possible way in which a man can be compelled to do his work willingly and when he does it unwillingly he is far from being efficient. He must have the opportunity to enjoy his work and realize himself in its performance." "In our plant," he remarks, "we never made it a practice to determine arbitrarily standard methods for performing an operation, for we believe that the men who are actually doing the work have generally as much to contribute as the foremen and department heads in deciding standard practices; and because we give the workman the chance to have the most to say about the matter, he is willing to conform to the standard, because it really represents a concensus of opinion of the men in his particular group." It is significant in this connection to remember that he does not pay the men by special methods to get the return. "I am not necessarily opposed to piece work or task and bonus methods of payment. . . . We have been able to obtain splendid results without resorting to a system of immediate money rewards." He thinks it is better to pay the workers liberally so that they "can forget this economic pressure and do good work because of the joy that comes from the consciousness of work well done."

Scientific management like ordinary management as a matter of fact does not want to cultivate initiative in the rank and file of workers; it would like to find more of it; and its eternal expectation is that enough of it will rise out of the oppressive atmosphere of the factory system to supply its limited needs. Scientific management especially wants this, as it must have more foremen and teachers to carry forward its advanced schemes of organization. But every manager will tell you that industry does not produce men with sufficient initiative to fill these positions. Their estimates of the number of men found in industry who have initiative varies from one to five per cent. The rest they believe are born, routine workers. They speak of their limitations as native. Managers do not stop to consider that their judgments are based wholly on the reaction of the mass of wage workers to the special stimuli which they offer. They say also that high school and college boys show up very little if any better in respect to initiative than the lower school product. The truth is that schools and colleges are more concerned with passing on the standards of an older generation to a younger, and the younger that generation is the less it is entrusted with opportunity to make its own first hand inquiries. That is, the lower schools which deal with a generation at its most plastic time, furnish the higher schools with minds inured to the pressure of accepting subject matter without independent inquiry or curiosity.

Factory management like college and school management, instead of depending on the subject matter to interest the workers, instead of opening up to them the factors of interest in industrial enterprise, has adopted incentives for getting the required work done. Enlightened school practice, out of long failure to get the children's initiative by the artificial stimulus of rewards for work done, now depends upon the content of the subject matter and the children's experiments with it, to develop their desire to do the work. The practice of depending on school rewards instead of interest in subject matter is largely responsible for superficial knowledge and lack of ability to think as well as to act. As schools fail to incite the interest of the children they train them to put through this and that task and reward them for it without having added to their power of undertaking tasks on their own account. Indeed, as they fail to give them the chance to do that, they actually decrease whatever power they may have had.

The doing of tasks in factories for the sake of rewards, gives the workers experience in winning rewards. As they are interested only in the reward, they carry away no desire or interest in the work experience. As the method of doing the work is prescribed in every detail and their only requirement, under scientific management, is to follow directions with accuracy, they are trained to do their tasks as the children in school are trained. They are trained in routine, and to do each task as it is given. This is not education, it is training to do tricks. The worker does not take over what can be called experience from one task to another. He forms certain motor habits, called skill. But under the efficient methods of scientific management the acquirement of this skill is robbed even of the educational value that it had under the unscientific method of factory work, which within its limited field, left the worker to discover by trial and error what were the best methods of getting results. Moreover, the standards of workmanship which scientific management sets up are not the worker's own standards; he has had no part in the making of them or in deciding on the comparative merits of the results. He accomplishes the results as he follows directions, not for the sake of the result, not for the sake of good workmanship, but for the reward.

As I have said scientific management has given the subject of incentives the same careful thought that it has given to the study of lost energy. The two important incentives for inducing the response of labor to productive enterprises which scientific management has carried forward in their applications, are wages and promotion. The general assumption is that the wage as an incentive has no limitations, except the physical limitation of a human being in response to stimulus. And surely it is true that the chance to "make money" is to-day the most powerful stimulus in use. But thoughtful managers of industrial enterprise tell you, incredible as it may seem, that the worker's objection to applying himself to his task is not invariably overcome by anticipation of the wage return; he will slack or be perverse or throw over a job in the face of opportunities to earn as good a wage or a better one than he can get elsewhere. It is well known that workers join unions in the face of opposition of employers and at the risk of losing permanent positions.

A resourceful manager in one of the most intelligently managed plants in the United States told me that women were less susceptible than men to the wage incentive. He found that many of them are content when their wage covers a sum which represents for them their personal requirements; that they cannot interest them in trying for more. On that account the manager takes up the case of the individual girl to see if her ambition to earn more money cannot be stimulated. They find sometimes that a mother requires her daughter to give in her whole wage at the end of the week and that the girl has no pleasure in the spending of it; they visit the mother and persuade her to let the girl keep a proportion of her wage and point out to the mother that she is limiting the girl's ambition. They also find girls who have entire control over the spending of their wages, who are without ambition to earn over and above a certain sum because that sum will meet their own recognized needs. The case of these girls the management tries to cover by encouraging them to save for vacations and other purposes which they offer by way of suggestion.

In both of these instances the management undertakes to create new wants or ways of realizing wants which were not recognized by the workers themselves. The satisfaction of these wants may or may not be in the direction of extending experience and expanding contacts. But that is neither here nor there. The point is, the manager of the industry has used an incentive for increasing production which has no relation to production itself. He is forced to do this because he fails to make the process of production a matter of interest to the worker. The processes of production do not of themselves as we know compel the workers' application or stimulate their desire for productive enterprise.

It is in the nature of the case impossible to increase the wage incentive indefinitely. One large and scientifically managed plant has made remarkable provisions for staving off the time when the dead line is reached. They have taken stock account of the labor power they require, the amount of energy which each worker possesses, for the purpose of evaluation and payment. They have undertaken to cover as separate items each condition which affects a worker's relation to his job. They rate as sep-

arate items the worker's proficiency, reliability,
continuity in service, indirect charges, increased
cost of living, and periods of lay-off; they rate
him according to the number of technical processes he is proficient in, whether or not he is
engaged on more than one; they rate him if he
attends the night school connected with the
factory and shows in this way a disposition to
learn other operations than those he already
knows. Why, they wonder, does only ten per
cent of the force take advantage of the school
and what, they are eager to find out, can they
do further to secure the men's coöperation.
For "coöperation," they say, "in a special way
deserves credit, since it is unexpected . . . certain well defined acts of coöperation will bring
extra reward." Their rewards so carefully
calculated did not seem to enlist response as
spiritual in its nature as coöperation. It
seemed that they had reached "the dead line"
where wage stimulus fails to draw its hoped for
response.

To get from the workers the highest efficiency
the scientifically managed plants pay for a task
a stated rate based on piece or time; if the task
is performed within the time set and the directions for doing the task as laid out by the man-

agement, are followed, the worker receives in addition to the regular rate, a bonus. Mr. H. L. Gant, while working with Mr. Taylor, discovered that there was weakness in the system of paying bonuses, and the weakness was not overcome until he devised a method of paying the workman for the time allowed plus a percentage of that time according to what he did. This method he declares constantly induced further effort and overcame what they discovered was the weakness in a flat bonus. As fair or as superior as this bonus may be in relation to the prevailing rate in the market, managers say that the workers are apt in time to fall below the standard as their work becomes routine, unless the incentive after a time is increased or changed in character. In other words the wage incentive is like a virus injection. The dose is not continuously effective, except as the amount is increased or altered.

A usual method of keeping alive the financial incentive is profit sharing and schemes for participation in profits, but they are rewards of general merit and bids for continuity of service; they have no direct relation to the workers' efficiency and compliance with standards which distinguish the wage rewards of scientifically managed plants.

Promotion, the incentive second in importance to the wage incentive, is of assistance in postponing the time when the dead line for the worker is reached. Nothing better illustrates the limitations of promotion in this respect than the fact that in factories where the turnover is the lowest, the opportunity to promote the workers decreases; it falls in proportion to the length of their term of service. That is, chances for promotion are the lowest in factories where conditions otherwise are favorable to the worker. In the factory where the turnover is only 18 per cent the management says that promotion is a negligible factor. Where the turnover is high there is greater opportunity in plants scientifically managed than in others to promote men, as the scheme of organization calls for a larger number of what they call "functionalized foremen" and teachers in proportion to the working force.

It is as I have said, on account of the necessity of these positions in the general scheme that managers of factories are interested in finding more men who have initiative, than industry under their direction has produced.

Before scientific management was discovered, business management and machinery already had robbed industry of productive incentives, of the real incentive to production; a realization on the part of the worker of its social value and his appreciation of its creative content. All that was left for scientific management to gather together for its direction were bits of experience which workers gained by their own experimental efforts at how best to handle tools. Their efforts it is true were not sufficiently great in this direction to promise progressive industrial advance. The margin for experiment which was still theirs was not sufficiently large to insure continued effort inspired by an interest in the work.

When we have taken into full account the repressive effect of scientific management on initiative, we may well admit an advantage: educationally speaking, the repression is direct. The workers are fully aware that they are doing what some one else requires of them. They are not under the delusion that they are acting on their own initiative. They are being managed and they know it and all things being equal (which they are not) they do not like it. The responsibility they may clearly see and feel rests with them to find a better scheme for carrying industry forward. The methods of scientific management are calculated to incite not only open criticism from the workers but to suggest that efficient industry is a matter of learning, and that learning is a game at which all can play, if the opportunity is provided.

Scientific managers have hoped that their plans to conserve energy and increase the wage in relation to expenditure of energy would meet little opposition. They also have hoped that the paternalistic feature of welfare work would allay opposition. But I am not inclined to include the welfare schemes in a consideration of scientific management; they have little light to throw on what educational significance there is in the efficiency methods which scientific management has introduced in industry. The playgrounds attached to factories, the indoor provisions for social activity, the clubs, while not having an acknowledged relation to the scientific management of the factory and while repudiated by some managers, are a common feature of plants which claim to be scientifically managed. There are scientifically managed plants which object to the recreational and other features which have to do with matters outside the province of the factory, on the ground that it is a meddling with the personal side of people's lives. "A baseball game connected with the factory," said the educational manager of a certain plant, "has the effect of limiting the workers' contacts; it is much better for them, as it is for every one, not to narrow their relationships to a small group, but to play ball with the people of the town." It is significant that this concern deals with the union and conforms to its regulations. Whether this more generous concept of the workers' lives yields more in manufactured goods than one that confines the activity of the workers to the factory in which they labor, scientific management, so far as I know, has not discovered.

The very nature of the welfare schemes suggests that they are inspired more out of fear of the workers' freedom of contact than launched on account of comparative findings which relate strictly to the economy of labor power. The policy of leaving the workers free, it was clear in the instance just cited, had been adopted out of a personal preference for freedom in relationships. The introduction of clinics, rest rooms, restaurants, sanitary pro-

visions, and all arrangements relating directly
to the workers' health have a bearing on efficiency and productivity which is well recognized
and probably universally endorsed by efficiency
managers, even if they are not invariably
adopted.

Scientific management wants two things;
more men in the labor market to fill the positions of functionalized foremen, more men than
modern industrial society has produced; and
it wants an army of workers who will follow
directions, follow them as one of the managers
said, as soldiers follow them. It wants this
army to be endowed as well with the impulse
to produce. It may by its methods realize one
of its wants, that is, an army of workers to
follow directions; but as it succeeds in this,
as it is successful in robbing industry of its content, and as it reduces processes to routine, it
will limit its chances to find foremen who have
initiative and it will fail to get from workers
the impulse to produce goods.

During the last four years, under the stress
of a consuming war every stimulus employed by
business management for speeding up production has been advanced. Organized efficiency in
the handling of materials has increased the out-

put, as increased rewards to capital and labor have stimulated effort. But the quantitative demand of consumption requirements is insatiable. It is not humanly possible under the present industrial arrangements to satisfy the world's demand for goods, either in time of war or peace. It was never more apparent than it is now, that an increase in a wage rate is a temporary expedient and that wage rewards are not efficient media for securing sustained interest in productive enterprise. It is becoming obvious that the wage system has not the qualifications for the coördination of industrial life. As the needs of the nations under the pressure of war have brought out the inefficiencies of the economic institution, it has become sufficiently clear to those responsible for the conduct of the war and to large sections of the civil population, that wealth exploitation and wealth creation are not synonymous; that the production of wealth must rest on other motives than the desire of individuals to get as much and give as little as particular situations will stand.

In England and in the United States, where the individualistic conception of the industrial life has been an inherent part of our national philosophy, the governments, with cautious reservations, have assumed responsibilities which had been carried in normal times by business. Because business administration had been dependent for its existence on a scheme of profiteering it is not in the position where it can appeal to labor to contribute its productive power in the spirit of patriotic abandon. But governments as they have taken over certain industrial responsibilities are in a better position to make such appeals to capital as well as to labor.

The calculable effect of the appeal to capital to assume the responsibility is in the long run of passing importance, as under the present business arrangement that is the position capital occupies. In other words, the appeal will mark no change in capitalist psychology as it promises to do in the case of labor.

The calculable effect on labor psychology may have revolutionary significance. It is quite another sort of appeal in its effect from the stereotyped and familiar one of employers to labor to *feel* their responsibility. That appeal never reached the consciousness of working men for the reason that it is impossible to feel responsible or to be responsible where there is no chance of bearing the responsibility. Experiencing responsibility in industry means nothing more nor less than sharing in the decisions, the determination of procedure, as well as suffering from the failure of those decisions and participating in their successful eventuation. As the governments in the present case have made their appeals to labor they have carried the suggestion of partnership in responsibility because the government is presumably the people's voice and its needs also presumably are the common needs and not the special interests of individuals. It is hardly necessary to point out that it was not the intention of government officials who made the appeal to excite a literal interpretation; they did not expect to be taken so seriously and up to date they have not been taken more seriously than they intended by American labor. All they mean and what they expect to gain, is what employers have meant and wanted; that is labor's surrender of its assumed right to strike on the job, its surrender of its organized time standards and its principle of collective bargaining. But when officials speak in the name of a government what they mean is unimportant; what it means to the people to have them speak, and the people's interpretation of what they say, is the important matter.

These appeals of the governments in this time of war to the working people have the tendency to clear the environment of the suggestion that common labor, that is the wage earning class (as distinguished from salaried people, employers and the profiteers pure and simple) are incompetent to play a responsible part in the work of wealth production. A responsible part does not mean merely doing well a detached and technical job; it means facing the risks and sharing in the experimental experience of productive enterprise as it serves the promotion of creative life and the needs of an expanding civilization. As the appeals of the governments at this time bear the stamp of a nation's will, its valuation and respect for common labor, there is the chance, it seems, that they may carry to the workers the energizing thought that *all* the members of the industrial group must assume, actually assume, responsibility for production, if production is to advance. Equally important in the interest of creative work is the power of these appeals to shift the motive for production from the acquisitive to the creative impulse. In the midst of the world's emergency, driven by the fear of destruction the nations have turned instinctively to the *unused* creative force in human and common labor, that is to the ability of the wage earner to think and plan. If the response of labor is genuine, if with generous abandon it releases its full productive energy, it is quite certain as matters now stand that neither the governments nor the financiers are prepared to accept the consequence.

If labor in answer to these appeals gains the confidence that it is competent to carry industrial responsibility, or rather that common labor, together with the trained technicians in mechanics and industrial organization are competent *as a producing group* to carry the responsibility, one need we may be sure will be eliminated which has been an irritating and an unproductive element in industrial life; I mean the need the workers have had for the cultivation of class isolation. As the workers become in the estimation of a community and in their own estimation, responsible members of a society, their more rather than less abortive effort to develop class feeling in America, will disappear. Under those conditions concerted class action will be confined to the employers of labor and the profiteers, who will be placed in the position of proving their value and their place in the business of wealth creation. On this I believe we may count, that labor will drop its defensive program for a constructive one, as it comes to appreciate its own creative potentiality.

Judging from recent events in England, where the government appeals to labor have had longer time to take effect, it seems that new brain tracks in labor psychology have actually been created. English labor apparently is beginning to take the impassioned appeals of its government seriously and is making ready to assume the responsibility for production. The resolutions adopted by the Labor Party at its Nottingham Conference in November in 1917 covered organized labor's usual defense program relating to wage conditions. The Manifesto which was issued was first of all a political document, written and compiled for campaign purposes. But the significance of the party's action is the new interpretation which it is beginning to give industrial democracy. It is evident where state ownership is contemplated that the old idea that industry would pass under the administrative direction of government officials, is replaced by the growing intention and desire of labor to assume responsibility for administration whether industry is publicly or privately owned. The Party stands for the "widest possible participation both economic and political . . . in industry as well as in government." In explanation of the Manifesto, the leader of the Party is quoted in the Manchester Guardian as saying, that when labor now speaks of industrial democracy it no longer means what it did before the war; it does not mean political administration of economic affairs; it means primarily industrial self-government.

Perhaps an even better evidence of the intention of English labor in this direction is the movement towards decentralization in the trade union organization. This movement, known as the "shop-stewards" movement is essentially an effort of the men in the workshops to assume responsibility in industrial reconstruction after the war, a responsibility which they have heretofore under all circumstances delegated to representatives not connected directly with the work in the shops. As these representatives were isolated from actual problems of work-

shop production and alien therefore to the
problems in their technical and specific application, they were incapable of functioning efficiently as agents of productive enterprise.
This "shop stewards" movement recognizes
and provides for the interdependence of industrial interests, but at the same time it concerns
itself with the competent handling of specific
matters.

Such organization as the movement in England seems to be evolving, the syndicalists have
contended for as they opposed the German idea
of state socialism. But the syndicalists in their
propaganda did not *develop* the idea of industry as an adventure in creative enterprise. Instead they emphasized, as did the political socialists and the trade unionists, the importance
of protecting the workers' share in the possession of wealth. They made the world understand that business administration of industry
exploited labor, but they did not bring out that
both capital and labor, so far as it was possible
for each to do, exploited wealth. That was not
the vision of industry which they carried from
their shops to their meetings or indeed to their
homes. Their failure at exploitation was too
obvious.

An interesting illustration of what would happen in the ranks of the syndicalists if the business idea of labor's intellectual and emotional incapacity for functioning, gave way before a community's confidence in the capacity of labor—we have in the case of the migratory workers in the harvesting of our western crops. The harvesters who follow the crops with the seasons from the southern to the northern borders of the United States and into Canada are members of the most uncompromisingly militant organization of syndicalists, The Industrial Workers of the World. On an average it takes ten years for these harvesters to become skilled workers and these men, members of this condemned organization, are the most highly skilled harvesters in the country. On account of their revolutionary doctrines and their combined determination to reap rewards as well as crops, they are considered and treated like outlaws, and outlaws of the established order they are in spirit. When the owners of the farms of North Dakota realized that their own returns on the harvests were diverted in the marketing of their grain, they combined for protection against the grain exchanges and the elevator trusts. While developing their movement they discovered that the natural alliance for their organization to make was with the men who were involved with them in the production of grain. And as the farmers have accepted the harvesters as partners they have formed in effect a coördinated producing combination. Without finally settling the problem of agriculture, they have strengthened the production group and eliminated strife at the most vital point.

In the period of reconstruction the industrial issues of significance to democracy will be whether or not management of industry as it has been assumed by the state for the purpose of war shall revert after the war to the condition of incompetency which the war emergency disclosed or whether state management shall be extended and developed as it was in Germany after the Franco-Prussian War. Fortunately, these evidences of a new interest of labor in industry as a social institution, give us some reason to hope that we shall not be confined to a choice between business incompetency and state socialism. The evidence of the desire on the part of the labor force to participate in the development of production is the factor we should keep in mind in any plans for democratic industrial reconstruction. It is inevitable that an effort to open up and cultivate this desire of labor will be regarded by the present governing forces with apprehension. The movement of labor in this direction is now looked upon with suspicion even by people who are not in a position of control. The general run of people in fact outside of those who recognize labor as a fundamental force in industrial reconstruction, conceive of the labor people as an irresponsible mass of men and view their movements as expressions of an irresponsible desire to seize responsibility. They are the men who are not experienced in business affairs and therefore cannot, it is believed, be trusted. The arguments against trusting them are the same old arguments advanced for many centuries against inroads on the established order of over-lordship. But over-lordship has flourished at all times, and in the present scheme of industry it flourishes as it always has, in proportion to the reluctance of the people to participate as responsible factors in matters of common concern. Corruption and exploitation of governments and of industry are dependent upon the broadest possible participation of a whole people in the experience and responsibilities of their common life. It is for this reason that we need to foster and develop the opportunity as well as the desire for responsibility among the common people.

After the war, it is to be hoped that America will undertake to realize through its schemes for reconstruction its present *ideals* of self-government. As it does this, we shall discover that the issues which are of significance to democracy are of significance to education; for democracy and education are processes concerned with the people's ability to solve their problems through their experience in solving them. If America is ever to realize its concept of political democracy, it can accept neither the autocratic method of business management nor the bureaucratic schemes of state socialism. It cannot realize political democracy until it realizes in a large measure the democratic administration of industry.

CHAPTER III

STATESMANSHIP in Germany covered "industrial strategy" as well as political. Its labor protection and regulations were in line with its imperial policy of domination. Within recent years labor protection from the point of view of statesmanship has been urged in England and America. The waste of life is a matter of unconcern in the United States so long as private business can replenish its labor without seriously depleting the oversupply. It becomes a matter of concern only when there are no workers waiting for employment. The German state has regulated the conditions of labor and conserved human energy because its purpose has been not the short-lived one of private business, but the long-lived one of imperial competition. It was the policy of the Prussian state to conserve human energy for the strength and the enrichment of the Empire. Whatever was

68

good for the Empire was good, it was assumed, for the people. The humanitarians in the United States who tried to introduce labor legislation in their own country accepted this naïve philosophy of the German people, which had been so skilfully developed by Prussian statesmen, without appreciating that its result was enervating. Our prevailing political philosophy, however, that workers and capitalists understand their own interests and are more capable than the state of looking after them, stood in the way of adopting on grounds of statesmanship the German methods.

The American working man has never been convinced that he can get odds of material advantage from the state. His method is to get all he can through "pull," good luck or his superior wits. He could find no satisfaction like his German brothers in surrendering concrete interests for some abstract idea of a state. He could find no greater pleasure in being exploited by the state than he now finds in exploitation by private business. The average American values life for what he can get out of it, or for what he can put into it. He has no sentimental value of service, nor is service anywhere with us an institutionalized ideal. We judge it on its merits, detached perhaps, but still for what it actually renders in values.

In conformity with American ideals, wage earners look to their own movements and not to the state for protection. Their movements require infinite sacrifice, but they supply them with an interest and an opportunity for initiative which their job lacks. The most important antidote for the workers to factory and business methods is not shorter hours or well calculated rest periods or even change-off from one kind of routine work to another. As important as these may be, reform in labor hours does not compensate the worker for his exclusion from the directing end of the enterprise of which he is a part and from a position where he can understand the purpose of his work. The trade union interference with the business of wealth production is in part an attempt to establish a coördination of the worker which is destroyed in the prosecution of business and factory organization. The interference of the union is an attempt to bridge the gulf between the routine of service and the administration and direction of the service which the worker gives.

I do not intend to imply that the labor movement is a conscious attempt at such coördination. It is not. The conscious purpose is the direct and simple desire to resist specific acts of domination and to increase labor's economic returns. But any one who follows the sacrifices which organized workers make for some small and equivocal gain or who watches them in their periods of greatest activity, knows that the labor movement gets its stimulus, its high pitch of interest, not from its struggle for higher wage rates, but from the worker's participation in the administration of affairs connected with life in the shop. The real tragedy in a lost strike is not the failure to gain the wage demand; it is the return of the defeated strikers to work, as men unequipped with the administrative power—as men without will.

There could be no greater contrast of methods of two movements purporting to be the same, than the labor movement in Germany and in the United States. The German workers depended on their political representatives almost wholly to gain their economic rewards. Their organizations made their appeal to the sort of a state which Bismarck set up. They would realize democracy, happiness, they believed, when their state represented labor and enacted statutes in its behalf.

If Germany loses the war the chances are that the people may recognize what it means for the people of a nation to let the title to their lives rest with the state; they will know perhaps whether for the protection they have been given and for the regulation of their affairs and destiny they have paid more than the workers of other countries, who, less protected by law, suffered the exigencies of their assumed independence.

How much the German people depended upon the state and how much their destiny is affected by it is illustrated better by their educational system and its relation to industry than by any labor legislative protective practices or policy.

George Kerschensteiner, the director of the Munich schools, in his book on "The Idea of the Industrial School," tells us that the *Purposes and Duties* of the schools are to realize the ideal ethical community, and that this realization is possible in so far as the educational provisions are made from the standpoint of the ethical concept of each state. In America we do not think of the state as the embodiment of our ethical concepts. The state, as we know it, is one of the several instruments for realizing ends, ethical as well as material. The state is supposed to serve the common ends of all people. A state may be used, we are all aware, as an instrument, either by Prussian junkers or American business men; either may capture a state to serve their ends. But as a state serves special individuals it belies its professed reason for existence, and in America is in danger of falling from grace, so far, that is, as the common people are concerned. But when a state stands in the minds of a people as the embodiment of their ideals as it has in Germany, it must for its own purpose spend time and substance in purchasing the people's confidence. In assuming the place of guardian it must of necessity minister to the physical needs of the people. If it retains the people's confidence in its guardianship, it is incumbent on it to pursue this policy. It is incumbent on such a state to mould the people's ideas of what their needs are. The schools obviously offer the most hopeful media for the accomplishment of that result, and they have been used in Germany more effectively in this way than the schools of any other country. The German school system follows hard and fast preconceptions of aims and ends, and because of this it was possible for Germany to put over its own particular sort of efficiency.

As a first requisite of efficiency, Germany classifies its people, gives them a place in the scheme of things, and holds them there. By circumscribing within definite limitations the experience of individuals it produces specialists at the sacrifice of a larger human development. The classification of the people and the training of them naturally for the German purpose falls to the schools. The sorting out of individuals begins at the early age of ten in the elementary schools, when each child's social and economic position is practically determined. It is decided then whether he shall be one of the great army of wage workers or whether he shall fall into some one of the several social classes and vocations which stand apart from the common mass of wage earners. The children in the German schools, who are selected at the age of ten for a more promising future than the trades hold out, have more leeway in the making of their decision. But even these children from the American point of view are summarily disposed of and fatally consigned.

The telling off of children at the age of ten and assigning them to a place in the social scheme for life is not American in spirit, nor does it conform to our habits and institutions. But, it is complained, the American habit of taking chances is not efficient. The habit of letting children escape into life with their place unsettled creates confusion and makes calculations in serious things like industry difficult. Therefore, unfaithful to the development of our own concepts of life we are expected to emulate Germany and to determine the destiny of the child. Germany undertakes to eliminate the chances of the individual and the taking of chances by the state, while the American ideal is to leave its people free to make the most of each new exigency that life turns up.

At the age of fourteen it is decided in Germany what industry or trade the children shall enter, that is, the children who at ten are told off to industry. After they enter their trade, their special education for their job is looked after in the continuation schools as well as in the shop. Their attendance at the continuation schools is compulsory. This compulsory attendance does not only insure supplementary training for a particular job, but holds the children to the industry which was chosen for them. That is, a boy is compelled, if he works in the dining-room of a hotel, to attend the continuation school for waiters, until he is eighteen. He may not go to a continuation school for butchers if he decided at the end of a year or so in his first job that he would rather be a butcher, or that he would rather do anything than wait.

The continuation schools protect German manufacture and the national industrial efficiency against indulgence in such vagaries. A butcher would prefer to engage lads who have had experience in butcher shops and butcher continuation classes. Avenues of escape from jobs just because they are uncongenial are thus quite effectively closed together with the chance to experiment with life—the chance which Americans take for granted. But it is just this element of waywardness and the opportunity America leaves open for its indulgence among working people that makes labor from the standpoint of American manufacture so inefficient. For want of opportunity to put individuality to some account we frequently fall back on waywardness in an awkward and futile protest against domination.

While the German scheme of placing its workers is efficient in its own way, so also is the training for each particular trade. A child is trained first to be skillful and second, to quote Mr. Kerchensteiner, ''to be willing to carry out some function in the state . . . so that he may directly or indirectly further the aim of the state.'' ''Having accomplished this,'' he says ''the next duty of the schools is to accustom the individual to look at his vocation as a duty which he must carry out not merely in the interest of his own material and moral welfare but also in the interest of the state.'' From this, he says, follows the next and ''greatest educational duty of the public school. The school must develop in its pupils the desire and strength . . . through their vocation, to contribute their share so that the development of the state to which they belong, may progress in the direction of the ideal of the community.''

His assumption in defining the ''greatest duty'' is that the members of the state are free to evolve and will evolve a progressive ethical community. But after a child has passed through the hands of a competent teaching force which fits him successfully into a ready-made place, after he has accepted this ready-made place on the authority of modern technology and business, on the authority of the state and religion, that the place given him is his to fill; to fill in accordance with the standards determined by the schools and by industry—after all this, it is difficult to imagine what else a child could do but conform. He could do no more, thus trained, than go forward in the direction he is pushed and in the direction determined before he was born. This is not our idea of a progressive life.

It has been understood generally in America that Germany's preparation and classification of her future workers and their placement in industry, was more responsible than any other policy for Germany's place in the world market. British and American manufacturers before the war urged the emulation of German methods of education and a reorganization of school systems more in conformity with the German. The demand of the manufacturers for reorganization came at a time when intelligent educators in America were recognizing that some reorganization was necessary to bring the school experience of children into relation with their environment and with the actualities of life. The industrial education movement in this country was based on the German, and the German idea was the dominating one. The movement here has shown little imagination as it adopted a system foreign to America, instead of initiating schemes which represented the aspirations of a free people.

Herman Schneider, of the University of Cincinnati, has made one of the most intelligent contributions in the adaptation of the German scheme of education. He divides trades into two classes, which he calls energizing and enervating. In those which are energizing there is an element of individual expression and opportunity for self-direction. The enervating trades are wholly automatic, and induce a lethargic state of mind and body. His comment on the situation is: "We are rapidly dividing mankind into a staff of mental workers and an army of purely physical workers. The physical workers are becoming more and more lethargic. The work itself is not character building; on the contrary, it is repressive and when self-expression comes, it is hardly energizing mentally. The real menace lies in the fact that in a self-governing industrial community the minds of the majority are in danger of becoming less capable of sound and serious thought because of lack of continuous constructive exercise in earning a livelihood."

Professor Schneider undertakes to enrich
this barren soil by alternating the time of pupils between the shop or store and the school,
thus coördinating the worker's experience, with
the assistance of schoolmasters who go into the
shops and follow the processes the pupils are
engaged in and who see that the experience of
the week in the shop is amplified and supple-
mented in the school. The arrangement also
provides that the pupils shall be taken through
the various shop processes in the course of apprenticeship. The experience while it lasts
may have educational value for the pupil. But
in spite of what it may or may not hold, for the
general run of pupils it leads up a blind alley
because the apprenticeship does not fulfill the
promise which apprenticeship supposedly holds
out. That is, the pupil, when he becomes a
worker, will be thrown back into some factory
groove where his experience as an apprentice
cannot be used, where he is closed off from the
chance to develop and use the knowledge or
training he received. If, as Dean Schneider as-
serts, "we are rapidly dividing mankind into a
staff of mental workers and an army of purely
physical workers," and if "we cannot reverse
our present economic order of things," then any

apprenticeship, even this brave effort of his, is a
pseudo-apprenticeship and even in the most energizing of the trades leads the pupil nowhere
in particular. Even the skilled trade of locomotive engineering, which Dean Schneider
classes as the most highly energized of trades,
does not escape. As a spokesman for the
Brotherhood of Locomotive Engineers ob-
serves: ''The big electrical engines which are
being introduced in the railroad system are rapidly eliminating the factors of judgment on the
part of the engineer and transforming that
highly skilled trade into an automatic exercise.''

The one-time value of a trade apprenticeship
to a youth was that it furnished the background
for mastery of machine processes; but apprenticeship under modern factory methods can do
no more than make a youth a good servant to
machines. The Schneider system fills, as well
as can be filled, a scheme of apprenticeship in
conformity with the prevailing shop organization and requirements, but it is not a fulfill-
ment for youth; it is not educational. There is
no progression from apprenticeship to industrial control; no chance to use the knowledge
gained where opportunity for participation in

administration and reorganization of industry is cut off. The best of trades is a blind alley, educationally speaking.

However abortive such an effort as Dean Schneider's might be in giving workers opportunity to enrich their experience for their own reconstructing purposes, it offered the pupils more content and better training than the ordinary school drill in its colorless and vapid subject matter. This fact is necessary to bear in mind, but it should not obscure the even more significant fact that the blighting character of industry is due to its motivation, which is wealth exploitation and not wealth creation. All of the industrial educational experiments have succumbed to the fatalism involved in the adaptation of their experiments to that fact.

A staff of investigators, who made a year's survey of the industries of Cleveland with a view of determining what measures should be adopted by the school system of the city to prepare young people for wage earning occupation and to provide supplementary trade training for those already employed, concluded that the choice of occupations should be governed primarily by economic considerations; that even from the point of view of the school, educa-

tional factors could not take precedence over
economic. They said: "The primary considerations in the intelligent selection of a vocation
relate to wages, steadiness of employment,
health risks, opportunity for advancement, apprenticeship conditions, union regulations and
the number of chances there are for getting into
it. These things are fundamental, and any one
of them may well take precedence over the
matter of whether the tastes of the future wage
earner run to wood, brick, stone or steel.''

This conclusion is fatalistic, but it is a brave
one. It does not fall back on weak substitutes
for reality; it does not throw the glamor of history and the æsthetics of industry around
trades with the poor hope that they make up
for the content which is not there; it does not
foster the assumption that training in technique of industry or physical science can enrich, under the circumstances, the worker's experience to any important extent. It accepts the
bald truth that all the material classed as cultural will count for nothing of value in a factory worker's life in comparison with the highest possible wage in the most enervating of industries. It stresses this highly important
factor, as it should, but merely as a physical

necessity. There is vital education in the consciousness of self-support, in the consciousness that one is earning the living one gets. But under present conditions the educational experience of wage recompense is not so significant as it might be if it measured the value of the labor performed; if it paid the worker according to his needs, and if he gave in return for the wage according to his ability.

The Gary school system is a notable effort in public school education to fulfill children's desire for productive experience. It is in striking contrast to the German scheme as it is based on processes which have educational force and significance. In saying this I differentiate between training for industry and participation in the industrial activity which is an organic part of the life of the children and of the community. The children are an actual part of the repair and construction working force on Gary school buildings and on the equipment. As the children are involved in the upkeep of a school it becomes their school. They experience the responsibility of maintaining the school plant, not by some artificial scheme of participation, but by the actual application of trade standards and acquired technique to operations which have

for them and those with whom they live important significance. They gain in their work a
first hand knowledge of industrial processes
and activity. In conjunction with skilled mechanics they work on the carpentry, the plumb-
ing, the masonry, the installation of electricity
used in the school building. They do the school
printing and accounting.

The children's life in these schools is an experience in industry where there is nothing
to hide, no trade secrets to keep back. The children have the full opportunity of seeing theiɪ
work through to its completion and understanding its purpose and recognizing its value
and use. It provides more than any other
school system a liberal field for productive endeavor. But the Gary schools are not industry;
they are a world apart; they represent, as all
schools are supposed to, moments sacred to
education and growth. They are not subjected
to the test of coördination in the world of industry. They give the children a respect for
productive enterprise that should be invalu-
able later in effecting their resistance to the
prostitution of their creative power. They do
not give them experience in the administrative
side of industry for which the children of high

school age are ready and in need. But in an admirable way they subordinate training in technique to purpose and give the children the experience of exercising control over their own industrial activity. As an industrial experience for children of grammar school age, it is richer than any other school system which has been developed.

The industrial education of Germany which was recommended for our adoption and which we have emulated to an alarming degree in our industrial towns, imposes prevailing methods of industry and technique of factory processes as final and determined. As industrial history and technique are taught in the schools, in effect they bind the children to the current industrial practice and to the current conditions. They stifle imagination and discourage the concept that industry is an evolving process. The effect of technical training in the German continuation schools (and the tendency is the same in our own industrial education courses) is to teach the children that the methods and processes as they are carried forward in the shop are *right*. No question of their validity is raised in the school. They are accepted by the children in the spirit of authority which the school

carries, as they would not be so finally accepted
by them in the shop. The impress of a developed curriculum, connected with an active trade
experience, that is, a trade in which the children
are at work, like the curriculum of a continuation school, is greater than the curriculum
which has been evolved for its abstract cultural
values. As the curriculum coördinates shop
and school activities and as it fails at the same
time to stimulate inquiry on the part of the
pupil into industrial or special trade processes as they are practiced in the shop, it becomes a positive, inhibiting factor in the intellectual life of the children. The perfection of
an industrial school room equipment with its
trade samples, its charts and maps, its literature, relating to the extension of trade and of
commerce, has the tendency like the curriculum
to impose on the children the weight of accomplishment, if this equipment is not used to stimulate inquiry and experiment in industry as
the ever fresh field for adventure that it is. But
the intention of these industrial schools is to
train the children in the acceptance of processes
and methods which are established. Nowhere,
in no country, has this intention been so successfully realized, because nowhere has it been so

successfully organized as in Germany through its continuation school system. And nowhere as in Germany are the people so successfully subjected to an institutionalized life as it has been worked out in the light of modern technology and business.

There are other and special reasons why the best of industrial education experiments in America have not met with greater hospitality. The average American parent still believes that a boy "rises" in the industrial world, not as they once thought through his ability as a workman. The men of their acquaintance who have been successful, have attained wealth and position, not as a rule through their mastery of technique or their skill in a trade; they have not come by their promotion merely on account of good workmanship, but through influence. It might be that they had had their "chance" through a relative or successful business man, or it might be that they "got next" to a politician, who required no other qualification than "smartness." A boy in a telegraph or a lawyer's office has a better opportunity to reach influence than a boy in a workshop. The scholastic requirement for such advancement as these

vocations contemplate, is provided for in the
established school program of the lower grades.
A certain display of a few historical and literary facts beside a facility in reading, writing,
and arithmetic are the qualifications which
average parents believe are the necessary ones
for their children's advancement. And, taking
the situation in general as it is, they are right,
and will be as long as the whole social system
discounts productive effort and rewards exploitation of productive enterprise.

Obviously false from an educational point of
view as these school standards are, they are true
to the facts, to the actual situation which the
parents have to face. The wave of popular opposition to a reorganization of the schools for
a preparation of the children for factory life
expresses the original conception of popular
education among sovereign people. The common school system exists, it is still assumed,
to fit the children to rule their own lives; to give
them an equipment which will protect them from
a servitude to others. Its ability to do this had
not been questioned a generation ago and,
theoretical as its original intention is to-day,
its traditional purpose to develop the power of
each child to govern his destiny, holds over.

If training children to read, write and count, training them in facts relating to history and language, did not, as it had been hoped, lay the world at the feet of the children, training them in factory processes, parents felt competent to declare, laid the children at the feet of exploiters. That is where in any case, in the light of common experience, they might expect them to land. To reorganize the schools with that possibility in mind was for the parents a surrender of their gambling chance.

The promoters of industrial education, with some success, have made it clear to the community generally that parents were giving heavy odds in their gamble, but these promoters would have made this more obvious to parents if they could have shown that the assets accruing from the new school curriculum increased more materially than has the wage earning capacity of their children. The results for individual children are not sufficiently striking to advertise the departure, and if they were, the departure would not warrant the endorsement of the community on the ground of the higher wage, as wages are fixed by competition. They are advanced by a general increase in productivity. But the increase that occurs through

more efficient methods in productive enterprise
is not a real increase; it does not relatively affect the social or economic position of the wage
earner.

In the last analysis, the wage return is not
an educator's criterion, in spite of the prag-
matic recommendation of the Cleveland Sur-
very. The Survey's recommendation for a reorganization of the school system is based on
the belief that the school is, or should be, an
integral expression or reflection of the life of
the community; that to function vitally it must
be contemporaneous with that life, as are all
serviceable institutions. As a school reflects
the life of a community it enriches the experience of the children and endows them with the
knowledge and power to deal with environment.
When a school system disregards, as our established system does, the entire reorganization
of the industrial world, it stultifies growth and
cultivates at the same time an artificial concept
of life, a false sense of values. The German
system of industrial education has recognized
the reorganization of the industrial world, but
this recognition has meant the sacrifice of individual life and development; it has come to

mean in short the prostitution of a people and the creation of a Frankenstein.

None of our industrial educational systems or vocational guidance experiments disclose the full content of the industrial life nor do they give the children the knowledge or power to deal with it. The general dissatisfaction with these school movements is that they neither prostitute the schools in the interest of the employers nor endow the children with power to meet their own problems. The training in technique which they supply has a bearing on the every day life around them which stories of Longfellow's life have not. But that technique, divorced as it is from its purpose, its use or final disposition, is as valueless as a crutch for a man without arms. An elaboration of technology through instruction in the general principles of physical science, industrial and political history and the æsthetics of industry only emphasizes the absence of the really significant factors. The conspicuously absent factors in all industrial educational schemes are those which give men the ability to control industry. No work in subject matter is educational which does not in intention or in fact give the person involved the ability to participate

in the administration of industry, or the ability
to judge the extent of his mastery over the subject. Industrial educational schemes, even the
best of them, leave the pupils helpless before
their subject. As they furnish them with a certain dexterity and acquaintance with processes
and a supply of subject matter necessarily
more or less isolated, the pupils gain a sense
of the power of the subject to control them,
rather than an experience in their power to
master the subject. The industrial school emphasizes the fact that the administration and
disposition of wealth production is no concern
of those versed in the technique of fabrication.

Many educators appreciate the lack of content provided by industrial school systems as,
with weak emphasis, they undertake to embroi-
der the system with history and æsthetics of
textiles or other raw material which the workers handle, or introduce the story of past processes. As this furbishing of impoverished industry fails dismally to add content, it succeeds
in emphasizing the actual poverty that exists.

Dr. Stanley Hall makes the suggestion that
books on the leading trades should be written
to stimulate the interest and intelligence of the
young who are engaged in industry or prepar-

ing to become the wage earners of the trades. In speaking of "the urgent necessity now of books on the leading trades addressed to the young," he says:* "The leather industry, particularly boot and shoe manufacture, is perhaps the most highly specialized of all in the sense that an operator may work a lifetime in any one of the between three and four score processes through which a shoe passes and know little of all the rest. Now the *Shoe Book* should describe hides and leathers, tanning,—old and new methods, with a little of the natural history of the animals, describe the process of taking them, of curing and shipping, each stage in the factory, designating those processes that require skill and those that do not, and so on to packing, labeling and shipping, with descriptions showing the principles of the chief machines and labor-saving devices, at any rate so far as they are not trade secrets; it should include a glance at markets, prices, effects of business advance, depression and strikes, perhaps something about the hygiene of the foot, about bootblacks and what is done for them, history of the festivals and organizations from St. Crispin and the guilds down, tariffs, syn-

* Stanley Hall, Educational Problems; p. 624.

dicates, societies, statistics, social conditions in shoe towns, nationality of operatives,—all these could be concisely set forth to show the dimensions, the centers of interest, the social and commercial relations of the business, etc. What is not yet realized is that all these things could and should be put down in print and picture, almost as if it were to be issued as a text-book or a series of them; all of this could be done to bring out the very high degree of culture value now latent in the subject. Just this is what pedagogues do not and will not see, and what even shoe men fail to realize; viz., that the story of their craft rightly told, would tend to give it some degree of professional and humanistic interest and dignity which the most unskilled and transient employee would feel. It would foster an esprit de corps, pride in membership and above all an intelligent view of the whole field that would make labor more valuable and more loyal. This material, once gathered, should be used in some form in all industrial schools and courses in towns where this industry dominates. It would bring a wholesome sense of corporeity, historic and economic unity, would give a touch of the old guild spirit and more power to see both sides on the part of both employers and workmen. Nothing is so truly educational in the deepest psychological sense of that word as useful information vitalized by individual and vocational interest.''

Dr. Hall's idea of a Book of Industry might have emanated from the heart of Mr. Carnegie. With the same benign detachment he seems to have mused at his desk about the shoe industry and the people engaged in it. It would not take more than a passing acquaintance with the girls and men in shoe manufacturing towns to know that if there was established a village library equipped with the history of shoes, the æsthetics of shoes, shoe economics, shoe technology, and shoe hygiene, not one of the girls or men who worked in the shoe factories would darken its doors to read about shoes. They would not for this simple reason: the workers' ''individual and vocational interest'' does not exist. They would say that they already knew more than they cared to about shoes. No literature could add culture or dignity to the job of stitching vamps for all·the working hours and days of a wage earner's year, while there is no experience of cultural value in the occupation, divided as the making of a shoe is into some ninety operations, and distributed among ninety workers. Dr. Hall's suggestion that a Shoe Book be written is a good suggestion but he must supply a better basis for a reader's interest than industry has given him, that is, industry as it is now administered. He cannot impose culture or dignity through books on a trade which is prostituted by business for profiteering. If the purpose of the Shoe Book was to create the glamor that was intended around the present day arrangement of making shoes, it would be a false contribution in schoolroom equipment; it would be as pernicious as other literature that introduced an artificial note into a real and living experience like industry.

The most romantic account of shoe making will do nothing to bridge the gulf between capital and labor as Dr. Hall seems so confidently to believe it should. The problem is not so simple or so easily disposed of. As Dr. Hall himself says: "As long as workmen are regarded as parts of the machinery to be dumped on the scrap heap as soon as younger and stronger hands can be found, the very point of view needful for the correct solution of vocational education is wanting."* Dr. Hall recognizes

* Stanley Hall—Educational Problems, p. 632.

some evils which are inherent in the present scheme of industry and which are antagonistic to growth, but neither he nor any of the advocates of the German methods of industrial education make provisions in their educational schemes for eliminating the aspect which contemplates the dumping of workers on scrap heaps. None of the advocates view the equipment of workers for industry in terms radically different from the terms in which they are viewed by business men; they offer them technique and matter of insignificance and indirection; they make no suggestion or move to open up the adventure of industry for the worker's actual participation in it; they accept the organization of industry which excludes their participation as an unalterable fact; even unalterable as an experience in the prevocational schemes of education.

National, state and local campaigns have been carried on in America during the last fifteen years for the protection of childhood and youth. They have been on the whole successful in their purpose to get children out of factories and stores and into schools. It was an embarrassment to the pioneers in the campaign to find that the children were against them; that they preferred factory or commercial life to the schools. The evidence of this preference was their wholesale exodus from schools when they reached an age where they were acceptable to employers or where they were not prevented by law. Back of the exodus, universal as it is, there is an urge of elemental force. A common accounting for it, the nearest at hand, is that parents of working class children are penurious; or that they are too ignorant to understand the deteriorating effect of factory life on children; or that they are too hard pressed in their physical needs to consider the best interest of the children. This reason given for the failure of the schools to supply children with matter of interest or significance to them, explained only why children did not want to stay in school; it did not explain their eagerness to enter industry. None of the reasons accounted for the zest of the children for wage earning occupation.

The failure of the schools to hold the children gave educators who recognized the artificial character of school curricula, their best reason for introducing matter relating to industrial life. The children's preference was indeed a valuable indication where reality or real sub-

ject matter would be found. The change off
from old school subject matter to instruction in
methods of industry was a logical experiment.
But the movement for industrial education was
not inspired by a watchful sympathetic observation of children's needs; it was in line with
the general theory, more or less accepted, that
schools should be a reflection of the children's
environment; it was in line with the demand
of employers for efficient workers either
equipped for specific processes or adaptable to
factory methods.

If the promoters of industrial education had
been observers of children from twelve to fourteen and sixteen years, they would have found
that as they left school they were eager not for
skill in technical processes, not for wages, not
for greater freedom of association in adult life,
not for any of these alone, but for all of these
as they were a part of the adventure of the
adult world in which they lived. "We have neg-
lected to study the most vital thing in the situation, namely the zests of the young . . . we
have not taken account of the nature of the
great upheaval at the dawn of the teens, which
marks the pubescent ferment and which requires distinct change in the matter and method

of education. This instinct is far stronger and has more very ostensive outcrops than in any other age and land, and it is less controlled by the authority of school or the home. It is a period of very rapid, if not fulminating psychic expansion. It is the natal hour of new curiosities, when adult life first begins to exert its potent charm. It is an age of exploration, of great susceptibility, plasticity, eagerness, pervaded by the instinct to try and plan in many different directions.'' *

Children of this adolescent time would respond more readily to school instruction related to the adult activities which held their interest and connected in some way with their own conception of their functioning in the adult world. Courses of study in processes of industry and practice in the technique of those processes would have actual bearing on the environment of which they were eager to be a part.

But instruction in mechanical processes and practice in technique of manufacture are the husks of industry when divorced from the planning, the management, the examination of problems, the determination of the value of goods in

* Stanley Hall—Education Problems, pp. 544-545.

their use and in their place in the market, the division of labor throughout an enterprise, the relation of all persons involved to each other and to the product. The schools with their industrial education courses do not undertake to supply their young people with an opportunity to plan; they are true reflections of factory existence as they eliminate all the adventure of industry, the opportunity for experiment and discovery; they do not satisfy the high impulse of young people to be of use, to be a part of the world of work. The spirit of the schools is preparation for something to come; the spirit of the children is in the present, and the present pressing impulse of adolescence is to share adult responsibilities.

The impulse of youth to take its place in adult life is exploited by industry and repressed or perverted by a system of education which fits the children into a system of industry without giving them the insight and power to effect adjustments. The actual job in a trade has satisfying features which the school lacks. It pays wages. That fact for eager children is estimated beyond its purchasing power. For them it is an acknowledgment, a very real one, that they have been admitted, are wanted in the big world where they are impelled by their psychic needs, to enter. It places them more nearly on an equality with the older members of their family and entitles them to consideration which was not given them as dependent children. They learn shortly of how little account they are to the boss employer but they are establishing all the time a new basis of contact and a new place in their personal relations; they are establishing it because they have economic value in the world outside of home as well as in it.

The industrial schools and the old type of schools are both adult schemes of getting children ready for adult life, not by experiencing it, but by doing certain things well so that they can be entrusted to do later on, what adults in their wisdom have decided that they are to do. But they fail to prepare children for the future as they fail to supply the children's present urgent needs. They use the period for ulterior purposes; purposes ulterior to the period of growth with which they are dealing. As they use this period for another time than its own, in effect they exploit it. Without consciousness of the fact so far as the children are concerned, the schools exploit this period of growth as effectively as the employers reap the profits of

child labor. Employers as beneficiaries have
more reason than the schools for diverting youth
from its own purposes, as they are under the
necessity of a price system which is competitive. The schools as well as industry use up
the placticity of youth; they kill off the eagerness of children to explore and plan, and cast it
aside for more consequential ends.

The consequential ends in America, we have
seen, have been less clearly defined than in Germany. Within a year, the United States has
become conscious as a nation of place and power,
conscious that it is to play a part with the other
states of the world. In playing this part, will
it retain its rôle of servant of the people, or will
it assume with its new world dignity the rôle,
if not of master, then of leadership? If still
servant, will it serve more efficiently than it has
our dominant institution, industry? If the si-
lent partnership between business and the state
is strengthened, will not the promoters of industry be in a better position than before to
appeal through the state, through the patriot-
ism intensified by our newly acquired world
position, for a more universal and a systema-
tized adaptation of workers in industry? The
schools in their disinterested capacity, disin-

terested, that is, in the profits of production, it would seem could be used most effectively toward this end. German manufacture made that clear to American manufacture before the war. It also must be remembered that it was Prussian pride for imperial position that inspired the complete and efficient surrender of the German schools to the needs of the German manufacturers.

America is, of course, "different." All peoples are. But so is our position in the world different from what it was. Our position is not now, nor could it be, the German position. Our past is different, and that will continuously have its effect on our future. But we are facing a great period of change, and the strongest forces in the country are the industrial, and the strongest leaders are the financiers. What the financiers and industrial managers most want is efficient, docile labor. The German system of education, in spite of the fact that we are different, might conceivably have that effect on the youth of this country. Under the pressure of industrial rivalry after the war, under the pressure of an imperial industrial policy, it may be that the people of the country will yield to the introduction of a scheme of education which it has been proved elsewhere can fit children better than any other known scheme into a system of mass production.

It is clear that industry could set up models of behavior more successfully in the name of education than in its own, and to the extent American children come up to these models the more employable they would be from the standpoint of business. If the pressure is sufficiently strong the people may yield to the introduction of a system of compulsory continuation schools similar to those of Germany. If they do, I believe they will eventually fail. But there is danger through loss of energy and loss of purpose in their introduction. Is it impossible for us to hold to our native experimental habits of life and attain standards of workmanship? Is it possible to realize the full strength of associated effort and at the same time advance wealth production?

Germany's industrial supremacy was due, as Professor Veblen shows, to the fact that machine industry was imposed ready-made on a people whose psychology was feudal. The schools of Germany, an essential part of her industrial enterprise, were organized on the servility of the people. We now know what building as Germany has built her educational and industrial system on the weakness of a people means. We are in the process of discovering whether in sacrificing the expansion of her people she can secure a permanent expansion of her Empire. It would seem the better part of statesmanship in America after the war to build industrially on the strength of our people and not on the weakness of another. It is the business of educators to point out the danger and to discover whether efficiency may not be gained in the country by giving children in their adolescent period the impulse for production and high standards of work, not for the sake of the state, but for themselves, for the sake of the community,—out of love of work and for the value of its service.

CHAPTER IV

EDUCATIONAL INDUSTRY AND ASSOCIATED ENTERPRISE

As capital and so far labor have failed to make industry an expansive experience it becomes, as Professor Dewey has pointed out, the business of educators concerned with the growth of individuals to cultivate the field.

If educators regard opportunities for growth with sufficient jealousy they will not wait for industry to emerge with a new program, or system of production; they will initiate productive enterprises where young people will be free to gain first hand experience in the problems of industry as those problems stand in relation to their time and generation. Their alliance should be made with engineers and architects and the managers of industry who have made themselves, through experience and training, masters of applied science and the economics of production. Engineers, not under the influence of business, are qualified to open up the creative aspects of production to the workers and to convince them through their own experience that that there are adventurous possibilities in industry outside the meagre offerings of pay-day. Mr. Robert Wolf is one of the engineers who is ready for the venture. He told the members of the Taylor Society that "scientific managers have not been scientific enough in dealing with this very important subject of stimulating the thinking and reasoning power of the workman, thereby making him self-reliant and creative." In describing the field in which practical engineers should operate, he laid stress on their giving large space to the originating, choosing, adapting power in men and the direction of it into positive constructive channels; to men's self-consciousness of their place in the great scheme of things.

This conception of the field of operation for engineers also described the field for educators. The latter have failed to seize the chance in the present industrial arrangement for the development of "the originating, choosing power" in the working man because they have been obsessed by the business appreciation of the working man's power of adaptation. It is because they labor under this obsession that they turn industrial education into industrial training whenever they include industry in their curricula. Educators know that there is adventure in industry, but they believe that the adventure is the rare property of a few. They believe this so finally that they surrender this great field of experience with its priceless educational content without reserving the right of such experience even for youth. They know, as we all do, that industrial problems carry those who participate in their solution into pure and applied science; into the market of raw materials and finished products; into the search for unconquered wealth. They know that the marketing of goods is an extensive experience in the world of men and desires. They are not alone in their lack of courage to admit that limiting this experience perverts normal desires and creates false ones. For the sake of education it is to be hoped that such engineers as Mr. Wolf may overcome the timidity of educators, and that, in conjunction with men capable of productive enterprise, they will undertake to give young people an experience which is not tagged on to industry under the influence of profits, but which is inspired by the desire to produce and the opportunity to develop the inspiration.

Before establishing a system of industrial education like Germany's, or extending the makeshift attempts which have been introduced here in the United States, it would seem well to undertake experiments which would stimulate the impulses of youth for creative experience, which would give them an industrial experience where the motive of exploitation is absent and where the stimulus was the content which the production of wealth offers. Such experiments would entail the organization of workshops in connection with schools in which the workshop experience was translated and extended.

Such workshops would be financed independently of the schools. They would not be financed on a basis of profits, but the capital invested would draw a legal rate of interest. The enterprise would be under the direction of managers competent in technological processes, in the estimate of costs, and the organization of the work on a basis of productive efficiency. The working force would be a corps of young people who had received their elementary school certificates and their certificates for employment together with the necessary

complement of adult workers for the successful
development of the plant. The working force
would be paid the market rate of wages. The
juvenile members of the force would be paid on
a half-time basis as they would work in alter-
nate shifts in the shop and in the school, so
that work in the shop would be continuous and
would run on full time. The exchange of shifts
between the shop and school would occur daily
or weekly or semi-weekly, as it was conducive
to the health and the intellectual experience of
the children and to the needs of production in
the organization of the shop.

The workshop would be devoted to the production of some marketable article or articles
which are simple in construction. The selection
of the product would not depend upon technical
processes of construction to furnish educational
subject matter. Educationally speaking, the acquisition of technique is a factor, but not a primary one, in the modern scheme of production.
The primary factors are those which have universal significance, that is which are common to
all industry, the relation of labor, of mechanical
equipment, of raw material, of the finished
product to the whole and to each other; the

relation of the market to productive effort and an effective organization of all of these.

The technical processes or their acquisition are of educational value, because they furnish the necessary experience for the evaluation and appreciation of workmanship; or would furnish a basis for such a valuation if the educational factors which are common to all industry were matters in which all the workers participated and were matters which they understood. It may be that there are certain mechanical processes which have universal technical significance and on that account would have special educational value, but even if those processes were determined and selected for industrial instruction and acquisition, it would not imply that those who acquired them were industrially educated. They would be industrially equipped to act as efficient factory attachments, but the acquisition of processes, even the fundamental ones we have had ample opportunity to discover, do not inspire creative interests and desires.

Because educational content in modern factory work is not accessible to the mass of workers, we have fostered the illusion that the educational subject matter of industry was inherent in the technical process of fabrication. As we have fostered this illusion, we have missed the educational principle applicable to the craft period, as well as to the present, that the condition of the educational requirement, is that workers' participation in productive enterprise coincide in the long run with creative intention and accomplishment. This central requirement of industrial education means that individuals learn to function with conscious creative intention in the environment in which they live and that their learning furnishes a basis for critical and informed evaluations in industrial activity. In the craft period the creative intention required the worker's mastery over every process of his craft. In this machine age of associated enterprise the creative intention requires the ability to associate with others in the administration of industry as well as to take the place of an individual in the routine of factory work.

For the reasons I have just stated the educational experiments I am suggesting could cover advantageously one of the many industries which are generally classed as unskilled, and almost any one of these unskilled routine industries would serve as well as another. Almost any one of the so-called child labor industries

could be made over into opportunities for young
people to experience the stimulating effect of
associating with others in a productive effort,
and gain the impetus which the stimulation sup-
plied to pursue their subject matter far afield
in general mechanics, science, economics, geography, history and art.

For the educational purposes of the experiment the selection of the industry would not
be made on the ground that the technical processes of one required greater intellectual activity than another; neither would the selection
depend upon whether or not the industry chosen
offered young people better chances than another for entrance to a trade where jobs, com-
paratively speaking, drew fair rates of wages,
or the economic conditions were in other re-
spects superior. The experiment would in no
sense be a trade preparation but an experience
where the enterprise of production was opened
up and the possibilities of creative life were
realized in association with others, so far as the
conditions and time allowed.

The industrial basis for selection of such experiment should hinge, first, on whether or not
the young people could function in the industry
advantageously to themselves educationally

speaking and to the industry socially considered: that is, whether or not the productive processes were in line with the capacity of adolescent children and the product was of social value; second, whether the product could be introduced successfully in the market and the enterprise become self-supporting.

At the present time, a proposition for the promotion of such an educational experiment is being worked out. Wooden toys have been chosen as the article for manufacture, because, first, the models were sufficiently simple in construction to make the work practical for young people who make up the work-shop staff; it is practical for the majority of the staff to range in age from 14 to 17 years. Second, the work done by Caroline Pratt on children's playthings has disclosed the fact that the present toy market is below grade from the point of view of the service of toys to children. The market does not supply the children with the sort of material and the sort of tools they require in their play schemes. Therefore, the product chosen has a legitimate social claim on the market. However, it would be valid, though not so interesting, if a certain sort of paper box which filled a legitimate trade need had been selected and a paper box factory had been set up as the basis of the experiment. As a theoretical illustration of my general thesis, paper boxes would serve better than wooden toys, because the latter product, as it is conceived, covers special intellectual content. But the particular sort of content is not a fundamental requirement for the educational purpose of the experiment. However, as the experiment is actually being planned in connection with wooden toys, I shall use the plan, as far as it is worked out, as my illustration. I shall refer later in discussing the school curriculum to the special intellectual content which the manufacture of these toys will represent.

After I set down the details of the experiment, which is now being planned for a workshop and school concerned with the production of play materials, I am hoping that educators and industrial managers may readily make the application to other lines of industry. The plan is tentatively confined to a two years' course. It may be found that two years is too long a time to confine the pupils to the work and the problems of the shop. It may be found in the first year that the pupils will be interested in following some of the problems not in relation to their work and in that case they would break their connection with the shop.

The working staff of the Toy Shop will include forty young people (twenty at work at a time in the shop) from 14 to 17 years who have received their working certificates and have left school with the intention of going to work. It will include also six or seven adults who will do the work on machines too heavy or unsafe for children to handle and who will help to supervise and direct the children in their tasks. The shop itself will equal the best of shops in point of equipment, safety and sanitation. It will not, however, like many of the best, elaborate these basic features in ornamental expenditures. The shop will present itself to the young workers as sustaining the best and most essential standards in use, but like all other problems connected with the shop, the best will always be presented as a temporary achievement which with sufficient attention can be improved. An important source from which improvements may be expected is the staff of workers who are in constant contact with the plant. In other words, nothing will be offered the workers in the spirit of final achievement, and the suggestion of completeness will be avoided. The opportunity to test out and appreciate the standards will occur in the shop experience, and the chance to achieve or experiment with other standards will be reserved, as I shall show presently, for the school hours. This will be the case with methods of work and with shop organization. During the hours in the shop the workers will be occupied wholly with their special tasks as they would be in any other shop, that is in any shop which had due consideration for the labor force; as much consideration as it usually has for the economy and the protection of the mechanical force would be considerable.

The workers may acquire the technique of all or of several of the processes. Their general facility in technique may contribute to their productive value in the shop or their mastery over several processes may have its educational value for them in relation to the industry as a whole; they may to advantage shift from one process to another to relieve the strain of routine work. For the sake of production and for the sake of the educational value to the workers, the shifting of the workers from one process to another will be a matter of experiment. But the workers will not be shifted from one construction process to another for the sake of learning all the processes because skill in all the processes is not a requisite either of education or production. The experience in the shipping of goods and in the handling of raw materials, in the installation of power, in the upkeep of the equipment and the general care of the factory will be participated in by all the workers in their turn, according to the requirements of the industry.

While there will be adjustment of the workers, and trials as to the place of each will be made in the shop, intensive experiments in shop organization, like other shop problems, will be carried out in the school. This arrangement will serve the educational and the productive purpose, as experimentation should not be limited by the requirements of the shop, but by the requirements of industry at large. The school will be indeed the workshop laboratory where problems which originate in the shop can be taken over for analysis and solution. These concrete shop problems will represent required school subjects as the progress of the shop and the success of the enterprise depend upon their solution.

Among these required subjects are:

First: The Technical Problems of Manufacture, such as (a) the receiving and the storing of stock; (b) making out orders for stock from shop orders and bills of materials; (c) planning operation and routing work; (d) standardizing materials and simplifying operations; (e) the elimination in loss of time in waiting for material; (f) the division of labor; (g) advantages and disadvantages of supervising in certain operations; (h) machine versus hand work and quantity production; (i) preparing and routing shipments; (j) making out bills of lading; (k) study of friction, loose belts, improper oiling, tool cutters and saws.

Second: Keeping the Financial Accounts and Estimating Costs. (a) Making out bills of materials; (b) calculating costs of material from bill; (c) calculating board measure and unit cost of direct labor and indirect labor; (d) calculations of power used by each unit of machine power; (e) calculating pay roll; (f) making out business forms, such as billing goods, invoices, calculating discounts; (g) paying bills by check, note and draft;

(h) business correspondence; (i) banking, depositing money, obtaining money on notes, discounting notes, drawing notes, balances of check books and checking up cancelled vouchers and obtaining bank balances; (j) time and call loans; (k) calculations and payment of interest on capital; (l) maintenance of sinking fund.

Third: Up-keep of the Working Force, Buildings and Equipment. (a) Heating, ventilating and lighting of the factory in relation to its effect on the workers; (b) valuation for each worker of his own physical condition and expert advice in regard to nutrition and other physical needs; (c) care of motors and mechanical equipment, care of belts, saws and cutters; (d) efficient installation of motors, sectional drive and individual drive; (e) disposition of sawdust, etc., study of exhaust fans and construction operation and function.

Fourth: The Economics of the Enterprise. (a) The market of the raw material—the study of the market in relation to grades, to cost, to transportation, to quantity in cost of purchases, to time of purchase; (b) manufactured product; selection of models in relation to their use and their art values; their cost of manufacture; relation to the selling price; the relation of cost to quantity and quality; (c) the relation of the rate of wages paid in the shop to rates paid in similar industries, to cost of production, to needs of the workers; (d) necessary margin of income over expenses for the up-keep of the plant, for its extension, for the maintenance of the sinking fund and possible contribution to the expense of the school; (e) the economic value of the school to the work of the shop.

Fifth: Art and Service. The shop will not depend upon the pupils in the school for models, but will welcome models which come from the pupils as evidence that the shop experience is a stimulating one. But it will be recognized that the pupils will have little to offer on account of their inexperience and that there is a world of designers from whom to draw and the shop is eager to command the best models which are obtainable. There will be a Jury for the determination of models to be manufactured. This Jury will receive certain instruction on the subject of toys, and will be responsible for making further study of the subject. But as has been pointed out for the last ten years by Caroline Pratt, who has given the subject scientific attention, toys are the tools of little children which they use in their effort to become acquainted with their environment, which they use in schemes of play, and which are in fact efforts on their part to try out and experience the adult life into which they are thrown.

Because this is true and the market is unsupplied with toys of serious value to children, the subject will be a matter for development and the introduction in the market of models which will serve the purpose of children in their play will be considered a matter of social importance and demand the serious consideration of the Jury. This Jury will be composed of the workers in the shop, the manager of the shop, an artist, and one or two people who have given the subject of toys careful attention. Discussion of the Toy Jury on submitted toys will center around, first, the value of the toys as tools to the children in their schemes of play, and second, around the art value. Both these points will entail much examination and thought. The first will involve fundamentally the subject of education, and the second, the technique of art as it is expressed through drawing,

color and design, but the decision in regard
to models for manufacture finally can not rest
on either of these fundamental points. It will
hinge on whether or not the models selected
are practical for production and whether they
can be marketed at a price which will cover
cost of manufacture.

The attention of the pupils will be directed
to the factory and school buildings and the
importance of making them a pleasant work-
place and an acquisition to the neighborhood
in which they are situated. The problem of
noise from machinery and dirt and dust from
fuel will be taken up as subjects demanding
generous consideration.

Sixth: Literature and History. Authentic
accounts and inspirational stores of industrial life, especially of the lumber, the wood-
working, and the toy industry will be gathered by the pupils and the teachers. Special
excursions, investigations, or general obser-
vations casually or unexpectedly made by the
pupils and teachers will be turned to literary use or historical record. The pupils will
be given full opportunity to write out state-
ments of facts they have discovered or to
write stories or plays or poety which are in-

spired by the subject matter they have gathered. These literary productions will not be called for as exercises in the art of writing or of fact-recording, but as contributions toward the equipment of the school. The books which are collected as well as the original compositions will be submitted to critical analysis and accepted as accessions to the library if they come up to standards in authenticity and in literature. The teachers as well as the pupils will submit new books or other matter and before they are accepted, they will be subject to the same critical analysis as the material submitted by the children. This analysis will be the literary experience and training as it will be participated in by all the pupils who are interested in this expression of their work.

Not all of this school work is incident to the success of the shop, if we measure success by usual business standards. But it is all incident to the development of a creative impulse in the individual, and it is incident to the development of industry as a socially productive enterprise. The fact that the school and shop work represent the planning and the decisions, that they

demand knowledge and experience, does not sig-
nify that the young people will assume to carry
more responsibility than they are capable of, or
that more will be expected of them than they
are equal to. It does not mean that their insuf-
ficiency will not be recognized and admitted.
On the contrary the accumulated knowledge and
experience of the adult workers and the teachers will be appreciated by the pupils as they
have the chance to make real and full evaluations. All the members of the staff will carry
on the work in the shop as producers and
learners and it is hoped they will carry
on the work in the school in the same
spirit. Young people will stand in the relation of partners as well as pupils to the
adults associated with them. If the school and
the workshop experience gives its pupils a regard for high accomplishment it will be un-
necessary to stress the fact that as responsible
members of the working staff the learners are
not on a footing with the expert workers. The
teachers or shop managers will help the younger
members to gain the knowledge and facility
which they have acquired as fellow members of
an enterprise in which all have a common interest. The participation of the young mem-

bers in the enterprise will be great or small depending upon their achievement of standards. For instance, in the case of office work whether the individual children are entrusted with the correspondence, bookkeeping or banking, will depend upon whether or not they have achieved the adult standards in the shop for such business details. But standards in business accounting, in estimating costs, in planning operations, and in technique, will not be maintained as they usually are in industrial schools for the sake of the training, but for the purpose of carrying forward successfully the actual work with which the shop is concerned. While the educational experience is concerned in part with appreciation of workmanship, creative inspiration in modern industry will never be a common experience until the workers gain an understanding and recognize the significance of their special enterprise in relation to other industrial enterprises and to the business of wealth production as a whole.

If the school experience is educational, the interest of the pupils in subject matter will not end with the solution of their shop problems or with their experience in industry. The above outline of tentative school subjects representing as they do the solution of the problems of a specific industry signifies merely the starting point of an adventure for young people in the serious affairs of adult life. There will be a large margin for choice in the election of subjects in which individual children will care to specialize but these subjects will be related more or less directly to the industry. The pupils will doubtless be freer in the second year than in the first to choose where they want to specialize as they will have had time in which to establish their ground work.

But the election of studies in a two years' half-time course will not admit of flights very far afield of the subject in hand and of the problems originally set up. Those children who find that their participation in a productive enterprise is an enriching experience may elect to follow some special leads in science, in the past and present history of manufacture and commerce, in economics, in literature or in art. The intention of the school is to open up opportunities for such expansive expressions of the concrete experience as time and the capacity of the pupils admit, provided that the expression has its valid relation to the promotion or the enrichment of the enterprise of which they are responsible members.

Certain pupils, we will say, will elect to carry further than others the testing of fuel, of heating and ventilating. Others may be concerned with experiments in power. A subject possibly will become of such absorbing interest to a pupil that he will want to experiment with the one he elects for its own sake and without relation to the problems in the shop. His interest may carry him into pure science, unattached to any problem in hand. In such cases the pupil should be given a chance to test out his interest; he should be placed on probation in relation to his elected subject and if his interest holds and is sufficiently serious he will be advised to give up the school-shop work and follow the lead his interest has taken in some other place or school.

Indeed the value of the experiment will rest on discovering whether or not it holds the interest of the pupils, or how and where it diverts it. The experiment is launched on the assumption that the normal adolescent child is concerned with the responsibilities of adult life; especially it is assumed that he is concerned to function creatively, to associate with others in

productive work, to help supply such fundamental needs as the housing, feeding and cloth-
ing and the pleasures of the world demand.
It is assumed that the desire for experience in
pure science, in art for art's sake, comes *before*
as well as after this period when the need for
social contact is, it is again assumed, the dominating emotion. We have no scientific proof
that any of these things are true, but we have
sufficient evidence to justify an experiment.

Whether or not it is possible for modern industry to offer young people a proper chance for
making their social adjustments is also a question which I hope this experiment may help to
answer. We can do no less than use the conditions of industry as they present themselves
to us as our basis for a trial. I have started
with the belief that possibly the division of labor and scientific methods of management if
handled by the workers in conjunction with engineers and people of experience can be made
the instruments of associated life. If there is
ground for this assumption it will be important
to induce the young people who enter the school
and work shop to give their industrial experience a fair trial and to postpone the pursuit
of pure science or art for its own sake.

The subject matter taken up in this school can be subjected to a formal school classification, under such regular academic headings as Mathematics, Science, Economics, Geography, History, Reading, Composition and Drawing. While these subjects will be experimentally rather than academically pursued, it will be a matter of small moment and short time for pupils to make up deficiencies which the traditional school courses require. This is true because the pupils will have had first hand experience with the subject matter in which the ordinary school child is trained or hears about. The free pursuit of their studies will give them a familiarity and speaking acquaintance with the subject matter with which the traditional school is avowedly concerned but which it handles and guards as though it were the custodian of some precious, but insubstantial matter, belonging to a world somewhat attenuated.

It is the intention of this educational experiment to bring down the great enterprise of industry, so far as it is possible to its real character and to high accomplishment, and in so doing to give the young people the experience of the industrial adventure and full achievement, lest they become the subjects of those

who control the movements of industry and
determine the character of its advance. The
practical test of the experiment briefly outlined
would be: (1) Was the creative impulse
aroused? (2) Were standards of workmanship
discovered and sustained? (3) Was a broad as
well as a working knowledge of subject matter
acquired? (4) Did the children approach established methods in a spirit of hospitality and
of inquiry as to their validity? (5) Did the
problems create sufficient interest to arouse the
desire and will to reject faulty methods, and introduce others of greater service? (6) Was the
enterprise a productive one from the point of
view of the market and an educational one from
the point of view of growth?

Such experiments educators and engineers
would enter together and together enjoy in reality the development of creative effort, which
is their profession. Such productive educational experiments in the absence of profiteering would give meaning to the early years of industrial life which now lead the children nowhere. They would give the young people, as
the experiments come up to the test, the spirit
for the adventure of industrial life, the courage

and desire for solving the pressing issues of their time.

If the claim made by employers were true, that from 95 to 99 per cent of the working force is without productive impulse, that this condition of development represents, as they say it does, the "native limitation" of the men who work, industry as a progressive enterprise is doomed and high hopes for civilization are without foundation.

If the position of employers is true and the limitations of individuals are as final as they have determined, there is nothing to do except perfect the mechanical responses of men. This preëminently would be the business of employers and not of education which is concerned with the growth of the individual. On such a basis, it is inconceivable that educators would concern themselves with preparing people for industry. If, however, these limitations are not native, but are due to some incompatibility between the institution of industry and the interest of the labor force, then the limitations of workers and of industry are a matter of paramount importance in the field of education.

As I have said before there is a common supposition among people who are not employers of labor, that such features of industry as the mechanical devices of modern technology and the division of labor in factory organization, are in their nature opposed to the expansive development of the people involved; that these features of apparent intrinsic importance to mass production, are antagonistic to individual growth and to the interest of workers in productive effort.

Without question, it is the business of educators to determine whether such features of industry as machinery and the division of labor are fundamentally opposed to growth or whether they are opposed only in the way in which they have been put to use and directed. We can discover whether or not these features are opposed only as the people concerned have the chance to master them and undertake, through their experience, to turn them to account.

Because industry has been impersonalized and the mechanics of associated effort in industry worked out in such large measure, it is to-day possible to conceive of spiritual as well as physical association in productive enterprise. A difficulty in the way of this conception, aside from the business complex, is our habit of thinking exclusively of creative effort as an individual expression. In describing the individual expression we would say that a man may create a machine but that when men jointly produce one they work. The creative act is in the conception of the machine in conjunction with its construction, and the conception, after our habit of thinking, is an individual and isolated achievement. As a matter of fact it frequently is. A man may create a machine if he conceives it and constructs it or if he conceives and directs its construction. Those he directs, those who do the work of construction alone, do not participate in the creative act, as the creative act is the concentrated intellectual and emotional expression and effort to produce an article or idea. The creative impulse is concerned with the transforming of a concept or some material into an expanded concept or a new object. The creative impulse itself finds its satisfaction in the process of completion and loses its force when the concept or object is produced. The use of the concept or object created is not a characteristic of the creative but of the social impulse. A man who is interested in the use or application of a product, the value it has for others, possesses the social impulse as well as the creative. One impulse is intensive and the other extensive.

But the creative effort is not *necessarily* an individual matter. It may be possible for a group of people to associate cordially and freely together with a single creative purpose and endeavor. It may be possible for each worker to experience the joy of creative work as he takes part with others in the planning of the work along with the labor of fabrication. It is a creative experience or dull labor as his association with others in the solution of the problem is freely pursued and genuine, or as it is forced and perfunctory.

My justification for making this assertion will be recognized by every one who has had the opportunity to attend shop meetings of a newly organized trade union. These meetings are unique as they disclose the force in a productive group, and the value of giving the individuals engaged in routine work the opportunity to pool their common experience and pass judgment on methods of work. Whatever decisions these workers come to, none are fully realized or freely pursued under conditions which industry imposes. But in the course of shop meeting discussions, it becomes

clear to an observer that methods of work is as
absorbing a topic as the relation of the work
to the wage. The routine which is the apparent
result of the division of labor, becomes under
discussion a matter of technical import. The
workers' knowledge of labor saving devices and
their resources for inventing new ones are as
expert as is the business man's knowledge of
how labor cost can be saved. This matter under discussion is of high interest and concern.
There is an integrity in the concern which evi-
dently springs from experience and the sup-
pressed interest in perfecting methods and the
inter-relation of the workers in a shop. The
vitality and intelligence of these machine ten-
ders may well inspire the agitator who ad-
dresses their meetings to curse a system which
withholds full knowledge of the workshop and
blocks the opportunity for eager workers to try
out new schemes born of intensive experience
and failure to function in the fullness of their
capacity.

Industry offers opportunities for creative experience which is social in its processes as well
as in its destination. The imaginative end of
production does not terminate with the possession of an article; it does not center in the prod-

uct or in the skill of this or that man, but in the
development of commerce and technological
processes and the evolution of world acquaintanceship and understanding. Modern machinery, the division of labor, the banking system,
methods of communication, *make possible* real
association. But they are real and possible
only as the processes are open for the common
participation, understanding and judgment of
those engaged in industrial enterprise; they
are real and possible as the animus of industry
changes from exploitation to a common and associated desire to create; they are real and possible as the individual character of industry
gives way before the evolution of social effort.

We speak of interdependence in industrial
enterprise as though it were some new thing.
The early interdependence had its roots in the
common knowledge and use of an inherited technology, where property was common in the
common use of it. Interdependence due to modern technology has increased, and the interdependence which characterizes our own time is
economic. The tools of industry as well as the
natural resources are owned, and only by application to the owner can a man live or labor.
However disastrous that ownership has been to

past generations, it has bound men together in their use of what we ironically call labor saving devices; devices which have not saved labor in the interest of labor.

Out of this close association of men in industry have grown our national and international business corporations and our national and international labor unions. These corporations and unions are transforming local and provincial relations into cosmopolitan acquaintanceship. The recognized value of the acquaintance is in the extension of knowledge of people through their use and wont of material things, of the ways and means of life outside limited and personal areas. The acquaintanceship does not imply friendship or sympathy or understanding among men or nations, it does not necessarily result in wisdom, and to date, it does not result in a larger social spirit. The acquaintanceship is based not on mutuality of interest, but rather on rivalry and misinterpretations.

While our institutional life is an acknowledgment that interdependence is a necessary factor in modern wealth production, we still measure the strength of a man, or a society, or a nation, and say of all that they are strong or weak as they are able apparently to stand alone. We have not yet discovered that a desire to stand alone in an enterprise where people are of necessity dependent, is a weakness and that our ability to coöperate with others in such an enterprise is a measure of our strength. "From a social standpoint dependence denotes a power rather than a weakness; it involves interdependence. There is always danger that increased personal independence will decrease the social capacity of an individual. In making him more self-reliant, it makes him more self-sufficient; it may lead to aloofness and indifference. It often makes an individual so insensitive in his relation to others as to develop an illusion of being really able to stand and act alone, an unnamed form of insanity which is responsible for a large part of the remediable suffering of the world."*

This provincial desire of individuals to stand apart and prove to themselves and to others that they are exceptional people is a primitive ambition in conflict with the actual facts of a present day society where interdependence is a law of living. This conflict is kept alive by the industrial motive of exploitation of people and

* John Dewey—Democracy and Education, p. 52.

of wealth. Exploitation precludes sympathy as it precludes growth. "For sympathy—as a desirable quality is something more than mere feeling; it is cultivated imagination for what men have in common and rebellion at whatever unnecessarily divides them." And further, Professor Dewey remarks: "It must be borne in mind that ultimately social efficiency means neither more nor less than capacity to share in a give-and-take experience. It covers all that makes one's own experience more worth while to others and all that makes one participate more richly in the worth while experiences of others."*

What Professor Dewey says in reference to the growth of children and adults is as abundantly significant in its application to society. "Normal child and normal adult alike . . . are engaged in growing. The difference between them is not the difference between growth and no growth, but between the modes of growth appropriate to different conditions. With respect to the development of powers devoted to coping with specific scientific and economic problems we may say the child should be growing in manhood. With respect to sympathetic

* John Dewey—Democracy and Education, p. 141.

curiosity, unbiassed responsiveness, and openness of mind, we may say that the adult should
be growing in childlikeness.''*

As America and the greater part of Europe
have been for over a century devoting their
attention to coping with specific scientific and
economic problems, is their manhood due to
appear? Is the raw, immature character of
present day association and interdependence to
be enriched by sympathetic curiosity, unbiased
responsiveness and openness of mind? In the
midst of this world war I venture no pre-
diction on the appearance of manhood. But
clearly there is a line of action for educators to
pursue. Clearer than ever before it is evident
that it is the business of educators to see that
schemes of education are introduced which do
not fit children into a system of industry that
serves either Empire or business, but a system
that serves whole-heartedly creative enterprise
as it might be pursued in the period of youth
as well as in adult life. Within the past century
and particularly in the past generation we have
made brave efforts at coöperation, but our fail-
ures to realize the spirit of coöperation are as
notorious as the efforts themselves. The effort

* John Dewey—Democracy and Education, p. 59.

to work together in industry has been brutal rather than brave. We shall account for this brutality in industry and recognize why the spirit for coöperation in other fields has failed, as we distinguish between a puerile desire of individuals to express themselves and their impulses for creative enterprise.

As industry through the ages has changed from the isolated business of provisioning a family to the associated work of provisioning the world, it has blazed a pathway for relationships which are socially creative. But art in social relationships will not be realized until a passionate desire for the unlimited expression of creative effort overcomes inordinate desires of individuals for self-expression. Art in living together is possible where the intensive interest of individuals in their personal affairs and attainments, in their social group, in their vocation, in their political state, is deeply tempered by a wide interest and sympathetic regard for the life of other groups and people. Art in social relationships is contingent on broad sympathies and extended relationships, and it is contingent as well on ability to work for social ends while remaining in large measure disregardful of the personal stakes involved. Because of our inability to lose our personal attachment for our own work, because of what it may yield us in personal ways, the world never yet has experienced the joy and creative possibility of associated effort. And because it has not we have still to experience art in social contact.

In group work there may be as much power to release emotional and intellectual creative force as in individual work; there may be more —we do not know. There is a tendency we do know in isolated, individual creative effort, *unless highly charged with creative impulse,* to cultivate personal equations intensively, limit relationships, and circumscribe vision. As the movement of our time is toward world acquaintanceship, the desire of individuals to limit their experiences for the sake of intensifying them, signifies from a social point of view as well as a personal, a neurotic tendency. There is a common and false supposition that the neurotic temperament is induced in the world of art. It is true that an art environment attracts people whose creative impulse is feeble or not sufficiently strong to sublimate the desire for intensive personal excitation. Such people choose art associations *because* they are limited to individual expression and not because of the overpowering necessity to do work which is creative. As the era in which we live represents a struggle for associated work and common interests and its highest concept is opposed to limited interests and autocratic rule, we may well give our best endeavor to realizing creative impulse in the field of associated effort, in the hope that the field of art will be some day coextensive with life, and that its expressions will not be confined to the limited world of sculptors, painters, musicians and poets.

WORK

Its Rewards
and
Discontents

An Arno Press Collection

Anderson, V.V. **Psychiatry in Industry.** 1929

Archibald, Katherine. **Wartime Shipyard.** 1947

Argyris, Chris. **Organization of a Bank.** 1954

Baetjer, Anna M. **Women in Industry.** 1946

Baker, Elizabeth Faulkner. **Displacement of Men by Machines.** 1933

Barnes, Charles B. **The Longshoremen.** 1915

Carr, Lowell Juilliard and James Edson Stermer. **Willow Run.** 1952

Chenery, Wiliam L. **Industry and Human Welfare.** 1922

Clark, Harold F. **Economic Theory and Correct Occupational Distribution.** 1931

Collis, Edgar L. and Major Greenwood. **The Health of the Industrial Worker.** 1921

Dreyfuss, Carl. **Occupation and Ideology of the Salaried Employee.** Two vols. in one, 1938

Dubreuil, H[yacinth]. **Robots or Men?** 1930

Ellsworth, John S., Jr. **Factory Folkways.** 1952

Floyd, W.F. and A.T. Welford, eds. **Symposium on Fatigue *and* Symposium on Human Factors in Equipment Design.** Two vols. in one, 1953/1954

Friedmann, Eugene A. and Robert J. Havighurst, et al. **The Meaning of Work and Retirement.** 1954

Friedmann, Georges. **Industrial Society.** Edited by Harold L. Sheppard. 1955

Goldmark, Josephine and Mary D. Hopkins. **Comparison of an Eight-Hour Plant and a Ten-Hour Plant.** 1920

Goodrich, Carter. **The Miner's Freedom.** 1925

Great Britain Industrial Health Research Board, Medical Research Council. **British Work Studies.** 1977

Haggard, Howard W. and Leon A. Greenberg. **Diet and Physical Efficiency.** 1935

Hannay, Agnes. **A Chronicle of Industry on the Mill River.** 1936

Hartmann, George W. and Theodore Newcomb, eds. **Industrial Conflict.** 1939

Heron, Alexander R. **Why Men Work.** 1948

Hersey, Rexford B. **Workers' Emotions in Shop and Home.** 1932

Hoppock, Robert. **Job Satisfaction.** 1935

Hughes, Gwendolyn Salisbury. **Mothers in Industry.** 1925

Husband, Joseph. **A Year in a Coal-Mine.** 1911

Kornhauser, Arthur, Robert Dubin and Arthur M. Ross, eds. **Industrial Conflict.** 1954

Levasseur, E[mile]. **The American Workman.** 1900

Lincoln, Jonathan Thayer. **The City of the Dinner-Pail.** 1909

Man, Henri de. **Joy in Work.** [1929]

Marot, Helen. **Creative Impulse in Industry.** 1918

Mayo, Elton. **The Human Problems of an Industrial Civilization.** 1933

Mayo, Elton. **The Social Problems of an Industrial Civilization.** 1945

Moore, Wilbert E. **Industrial Relations and the Social Order.** 1951

Morse, Nancy C. **Satisfactions in the White-Collar Job.** 1953

Myers, Charles S. **Industrial Psychology.** [1925]

Noland, E. William and E. Wight Bakke. **Workers Wanted.** 1949

Oakley, C[harles] A[llen]. **Men at Work.** 1946

Odencrantz, Louise C. **Italian Women in Industry.** 1919

Purcell, Theodore V. **Blue Collar Man.** 1960

Reiss, Albert J., Jr., et al. **Occupations and Social Status.** 1961

Reynolds, Lloyd G. and Joseph Shister. **Job Horizons.** 1949

Rhyne, Jennings J. **Some Southern Cotton Mill Workers and Their Villages.** 1930

Richardson, F. L. W. and Charles R. Walker. **Human Relations in an Expanding Company.** 1948

Roe, Anne. **The Psychology of Occupations.** 1956

Sayles, Leonard R. **Behavior of Industrial Work Groups.** 1958

Seashore, Stanley E. **Group Cohesiveness in the Industrial Work Group.** 1954

Shepard, William P. **The Physician in Industry.** 1961

Smith, Elliott Dunlap. **Technology & Labor.** 1939

Soule, George. **What Automation Does to Human Beings.** 1956

Spofford, Harriet Prescott. **The Servant Girl Question.** 1881

Staley, Eugene, ed. **Creating an Industrial Civilization.** 1952

Stein, Leon, ed. **Work or Labor.** 1977

Suffer the Little Children. 1977

Tead, Ordway. **Human Nature and Management.** 1929

Tilgher, Adriano. **Work:** What It Has Meant to Men Through the Ages. 1930

Todd, Arthur James. **Industry and Society.** 1933

Tugwell, Rexford G. **The Industrial Discipline and the Governmental Arts.** 1933

U.S. House of Representatives, Committee on Labor. **The Stop Watch and Bonus System in Government Work.** 1914

Vernon, H[orace] M[iddleton]. **Industrial Fatigue and Efficiency.** 1921

Walker, Charles Rumford. **Steel:** The Diary of a Furnace Worker. 1922

Whitehead, T.N. **The Industrial Worker.** Two vols. in one. 1938

Whitehead, T.N. **Leadership in a Free Society.** 1936

Whyte, William Foote. **Human Relations in the Restaurant Industry.** 1948